Google ⇒ More ⇒ Translate ⇒
Bulgarian ⇒ Bulgarian Key Board.

Phr

D1458376

BULGARIAN

With menu decoder, survival
guide and two-way dictionary

Thomas Cook
Publishing

www.thomascookpublishing.com

BULGARIAN PHRASE Book
ISBN 954 - 8805 - 23 - 5

Introduction.....................5

Greetings.........................9

Eating out.......................13

Shopping.........................27

Getting around................37

Accommodation..............43

Survival guide..................49

Emergencies.....................59

Dictionary.........................63

Quick reference...............94

How to use this guide

The ten chapters in this guide are colour-coded to help you find what you're looking for. These colours are used on the tabs of the pages and in the contents on the previous page and above.

For quick reference, you'll find some basic expressions on the inside front cover and essential emergency phrases on the inside back cover. There is also a handy reference section for numbers, measurements and clothes sizes at the back of the guide.

Front cover photography © Craft Alan King/Alamy
Cover design/artwork by Jonathan Glick
Photos: BigStockPhoto.com [Ivan Cholakov (p44), Nikolay Dimitorv (p42),
Michael Gray (p11), Štěpán Ježek (p45), Harris Shiffman (p17) and Ljupco
Smokovski (p38)], Neil Carey (p37), Boby Dimitrov (p25), Quinn Dombrowski
(p63), Bruno Girin (p5), Klearchos Kapoutsis (p32), Jerzy Kociatkiewicz (p27)
and SXC.hu [Steve Estvanik (p29), LotusHead (pp21 & 31), Robert Owen-Wahl
(p16), Teodora Vlaicu (p28), Steve Woods (p19) and Michal Zacharzewski (p26)].

Produced by The Content Works Ltd
Aston Court, Kingsmead Business Park, Frederick Place
High Wycombe, Bucks HP11 1LA
www.thecontentworks.com
Design concept: Mike Wade
Layout: Alison Rayner
Text: Polia Mihaylova
Editing: Paul Hines
Proofing: Monica Guy & Valentina Ibrishimova
Editorial/project management: Lisa Plumridge

Published by Thomas Cook Publishing
A division of Thomas Cook Tour Operations Limited
Company registration No: 3772199 England
The Thomas Cook Business Park, 9 Coningsby Road
Peterborough PE3 8SB, United Kingdom
Email: books@thomascook.com, Tel: +44 (0)1733 416477
www.thomascookpublishing.com

ISBN-13: 978-1-84848-105-3

First edition © 2009 Thomas Cook Publishing
Text © 2009 Thomas Cook Publishing

Project Editor: Maisie Fitzpatrick
Production/DTP: Steven Collins

Printed and bound in Italy by Printer Trento

Introduction

Bulgarian is no foreign language lite: it's the real deal, right down to the letters of its alphabet. Some look and sound just like they do in English; others look familiar but are pronounced differently; then come those that look like something from another planet – for example, Ф is an F, and what looks like the number 3 is actually a Z.

In cities many locals speak English, but this is not the case in smaller towns and villages around the country. Most signs and street names are in Cyrillic. So the more you familiarise yourself with this exotically beautiful language, the more comfortable you'll feel in Bulgaria.

Introduction

Bulgarian was the first Slavic language to be written down. In 855 AD two brothers, Cyril and Methodius, created the Glagolitic alphabet to translate religious texts. Its knotty letters were gradually superseded by the more user-friendly Cyrillic ones, thus forming the 30-letter Bulgarian alphabet.

Most of the words in modern Bulgarian come from very early Slavonic times. Some Turkish words were also adopted during the long period of Ottoman rule. Added to the mix is some Latin, a sprinkling of Russian and an increasing number of English words connected with computer technology. This heady cocktail of influences is given a twist by the fact that Bulgarian word stress is pretty unpredictable. Even better, the meaning of some words changes when you change the stressed syllable!

The basics

The first step in your Bulgarian language experience is to get familiar with the Cyrillic alphabet. Below you'll see the Cyrillic characters (capitals and small letters), the official transliteration into English letters, and example words to illustrate how they are pronounced.

Аа	a	as in	**a**go
Бб	b	as in	**b**ack
Вв	v	as in	**v**an
Гг	g	as in	**g**ame
Дд	d	as in	**d**ock
Ее	e	as in	l**e**t
Жж	zh	as 's' in	mea**s**ure
Зз	z	as in	**z**oo
Ии	i	as in	t**i**p
Йй	y	as in	**y**oke
Кк	k	as in	**k**ing
Лл	l	as in	**l**ove
Мм	m	as in	**m**ap
Нн	n	as in	**n**ot
Оо	o	as in	**o**dd
Пп	p	as in	**p**en
Рр	r	as in	**r**un
Сс	s	as in	**s**et
Тт	t	as in	**t**axi
Уу	u	as in	r**u**le
Фф	f	as in	**f**ace

Xx	h	as in	**h**and
Цц	ts	as in	cu**ts**
Чч	ch	as in	**ch**eck
Шш	sh	as in	**sh**e
Щщ	sht	as in	sma**shed**
Ъъ	a	as in	b**u**t
Ьь	softens 'o'	as in	**yo**ga
Юю	yu	as in	**you**
Яя	ya	as in	**ya**rd

Grammar

Bulgarian grammar will look very odd, particularly to those who have never studied another foreign language. Nouns in Bulgarian have three genders – masculine, feminine or neuter. Making a singular word into a plural (for example "cat" to "cats") depends partly on the word ending and partly on its gender, but can be unpredictable. The word for "the" is tagged onto the end of the word it's referring to, but again depends on its gender and on whether it is singular or plural. There is no specific equivalent of the words "a" or "an".

Adjectives, like "red" or "happy", usually come before the nouns they are describing (for example "red car"). Verbs also vary wildly depending on the sentence. Don't worry too much about the niceties of Bulgarian grammar – it is better to learn a few set phrases and a stock of useful vocabulary in order to make yourself understood.

Basic conversation

Hello	**Здравей**	*Zdravey*
Goodbye	**Довиждане**	*Dovizhdane*
Yes	**Да**	*Da*

Relatively speaking

Bulgarians have individual words for every relative imaginable. For instance, the terms for "uncle" differ depending on whether it refers to your mother's brother or to your father's. Imagine the guest list for a Bulgarian wedding!

No	Не	Ne
Please	Моля	Molya
Thank you	Благодаря	Blagodarya
You're welcome	Моля	Molya
Sorry	Съжалявам	Sazhalyavam
Excuse me (apology)	Извинете	Izvinete
Excuse me (to get attention)	Извинете	Izvinete
Excuse me (to get past)	Извинете	Izvinete

Do you speak English?	Говорите ли английски?	Govorite li angliyski?
I don't speak Bulgarian	Аз не говоря български	Az ne govorya balgarski
I speak a little Bulgarian	Говоря малко български	Govorya malko balgarski

What?	Какво?	Kakvo?
I understand	Разбирам	Razbiram
I don't understand	Не разбирам	Ne razbiram
Do you understand?	Разбирате ли?	Razbirate li?
I don't know	Не знам	Ne znam
I can't	Не мога	Ne moga

Can you... please?	Може ли... моля?	Mozhe li...molya?
- speak more slowly	- да говорите по-бавно	- da govorite po-bavno
- repeat that	- да повторите това	- da povtorite tova

Present perfectly ridiculous

The challenge posed by the grammatically correct usage of verbs leads locals to joke about verbs in the "almost possible but unpredictable future" tense and the "perfect, but not quite perfect".

Greetings

At first glance, Bulgarians appear quite formal. Initial meetings consist of a firm handshake, direct eye contact and the appropriate greeting for the time of day. Handshakes are used both when meeting and when saying goodbye. Address new acquaintances as Mr, Mrs, or Miss So-and-so. First names, kisses and hugs are used among friends or family.

Once you are accepted, the formal curtain will drop and you will discover that Bulgarian people are indeed very friendly and welcoming. You might even be overwhelmed with hospitality – be prepared for long dinners with endless toasts.

Meeting someone

Hello	**Здравей/те**	*Zdravey/te*
Hi	**Здрасти**	*Zdrasti*
Good morning	**Добро утро**	*Dobro utro*
Good afternoon	**Добър ден**	*Dobar den*
Good evening	**Добър вечер**	*Dobar vecher*

Sir/Mr	**Господин**	*Gospodin*
Madam/Mrs	**Госпожа**	*Gospozha*
Miss	**Госпожица**	*Gospozhitsa*

How are you?	**Как сте/си?**	*Kak ste/si?*
Fine, thank you	**Добре, благодаря**	*Dobre, blagodarya*
And you?	**А Вие/ти?**	*A vie/ti?*
Very well	**Много добре**	*Mnogo dobre*
Not very well	**Не много добре**	*Ne mnogo dobre*

Small talk

My name is...	**Аз се казвам…**	*Az se kazvam...*
What's your name?	**Как се казвате/ казваш?**	*Kak se kazvate/ kazvash?*
I'm pleased to meet you	**Приятно ми е да се запознаем**	*Priyatno mi e da se zapoznaem*

| Where are you from? | **Откъде сте/си?** | *Otkade ste/si?* |
| I am from Britain | **Аз съм от Великобритания** | *Az sam ot Velikobritaniya* |

Do you live here?	**Тук ли живеете?**	*Tuk li zhiveete?*
This is a great...	**Това е...**	*Tova e...*
- country	**- чудесна страна**	*- chudesna strana*
- town	**- чудесен град**	*- chudesen grad*

| I am staying at... | **Аз съм в/във…** | *Az sam v/vav...* |
| I'm just here for the day | **Аз съм тук само за днес** | *Az sam tuk samo za dnes* |

I'm in... for...	**Аз съм в/във… за…**	*Az sam v/vav... za...*
- a weekend	**- уикенда**	*- uikenda*
- a week	**- за една седмица**	*- za edna sedmitsa*

Noddy language
A confusing aspect of Bulgarian social intercourse is that "yes" is indicated by a shake of the head and "no" is expressed with a nod. Just to make things more puzzling, many young people now use the opposite European manner!

| How old are you? | На колко години сте/си? | Na kolko godini ste/si? |
| I'm... years old | Аз съм на... години | Az sam na... godini |

Family
This is my...	Това е…	Tova e...
- husband	- моят съпруг	- moyat saprug
- wife	- моята съпруга	- moyata sapruga
- partner	- моят партньор	- moyat partnyor
- boyfriend/ girlfriend	- моят приятел/ моята приятелка	- moyat priyatel/ moyata priyatelka

I have a...	Аз имам…	Az imam...
- son	- син	- sin
- daughter	- дъщеря	- dashterya
- grandson	- внук	- vnuk
- granddaughter	- внучка	- vnuchka

Do you have...	Имате/имаш ли…	Imate/imash li...
- children?	- деца?	- detsa?
- grandchildren?	- внуци?	- vnutsi?
I don't have children	Нямам деца	Nyamam detsa

Are you married?	Семеен/семейна ли сте/си?	Semeen/semeyna li ste/si?
I'm...	Аз съм…	Az sam...
- single	- несемеен/ несемейна	- nesemeen/ nesemeyna

- married	- женен/омъжена	- _zhenen/_ _omazhena_
- divorced	- разведен/а	- _razveden/a_
- widowed	- вдовец/вдовица	- _vdovets/vdovitsa_

Saying goodbye

Goodbye	Довиждане	_Dovizhdane_
Good night	Лека нощ	_Leka nosht_
Sleep well	Приятни сънища	_Priyatni sanishta_
See you later	До скоро	_Do skoro_
Have a good trip!	Приятно пътуване!	_Priyatno patuvane!_
It was nice meeting you	Беше ми приятно да се запознаем	_Beshe mi priyatno da se zapoznaem_
All the best	Всичко най-добро	_Vsichko nay dobro_
Have fun	Приятно прекарване	_Priyatno prekarvane_
Good luck	Късмет	_Kasmet_
Keep in touch	Ще поддържаме връзка	_Shte poddarzhame vrazka_
My address is...	Моят адрес е...	_Moyat adres e..._
What's your...	Какъв е твоят...	_Kakav e tvoyat..._
- address?	- адрес?	- _adres?_
- email?	- имейл?	- _imeyl?_
- telephone number?	- телефонен номер?	- _telefonen nomer?_

An attitude of gratitude

You often hear locals using _mersi_ for expressing gratitude. The usual response is _molya_, which literally means "please", but suggests "you are welcome".

Eating Out

Bulgarian cooking, which is heavily influenced by Turkish and Greek cuisine, is positively rippling with robust, no-nonsense delights. Well known national specialities include the herb chubritsa, while distinctive ingredients include *kiselo mlyako* (Bulgarian yoghurt) and *sirene* (white cheese), both of which are delicious.

A familiar sight on the dinner table is pile after pile of fresh and flavoursome vegetables grown naturally and prepared unfussily. In Bulgaria, nibbling on a stick of celery and whipping out your calorie calculator is out; filling your boots is most definitely in.

Introduction

With the exception of a small but growing band of eat-on-the-go professionals, Bulgarians take their meals at the same slow pace as they do life. Dinner is a ritual that always begins with salads accompanied by glasses of the local brandy, *rakiya*. The main course is washed down with wine or beer, and the dessert is optional. People then continue to drink, nibble and talk for a few more hours, the chat being as important as the food.

I'd like...	Искам...	*Iskam...*
- a table for two	- маса за двама	- *masa za dvama*
- a sandwich	- сандвич	- *sandvich*
- a coffee	- кафе	- *kafe*
- a tea (with milk)	- чай (с мляко)	- *chay (s mlyako)*
Do you have a menu in English?	Имате ли меню на английски?	*Imate li menyu na angliyski?*
The bill, please	Сметката, моля	*Smetkata, molya*

You may hear...

Smoking or non-smoking?	За пушачи или непушачи?	*Za pushachi ili nepushachi?*
What are you going to have?	Какво ще желаете?	*Kakvo shte zhelaete?*

How many slices?

No Bulgarian waiter will bring a basket of fresh bread to your table the moment you sit down. You will have to request it and possibly even state how many slices you require.

The cuisines of Bulgaria

National specialities

Bulgarians are great salad lovers, and no meal is complete without one (they're often a meal in themselves). Mainstays of any menu are grilled meat garnished with seasonal fresh

Smoke gets in your eyes
Although eateries are required by law to provide a non-smoking section, it will be surrounded by people puffing furiously away – in Bulgaria, smoking is an art form.

vegetables and thick stews flavoured with aromatic herbs, baked and served in earthenware pots.

Signature dishes (see menu decoder for more dishes)

Таратор	*Tarator*	Cold cucumber and yogurt soup
Баница	*Banitsa*	Pastry filled with cheese and eggs
Шопска салата	*Shopska salata*	Assorted veg sprinkled with cheese
Качамак	*Kachamak*	Cheesy white sauce
Яйца по панагюрски	*Yaytsa po panagyurski*	Poached eggs with yoghurt and garlic
Кебапче	*Kebapche*	Spicy grilled patty of minced meat
Сирене	*Sirene*	White feta-like cheese
Чубрица	*Chubritsa*	Summer savoury (a Bulgarian herb)

The Black Sea region

Unsurprisingly, fish is the main feature of most recipes in this region. It's usually combined with a lot of vegetables and spicy herbs, so food in this area is actually quite healthy.

Signature dishes (see menu decoder for more dishes)

Риба плакия	*Riba plakiya*	Roasted fish in spicy tomato sauce
Рибен гювеч	*Riben gyuvech*	Fish and vegetable stew

Скумрия на керемида	*Skumriya na keremida*	Spicy mackerel in a clay pot
Маринован паламуд	*Marinovan palamud*	Marinated belted bonito
Пържена цаца	*Parzhena tsatsa*	Deep-fried small white fish

Rite old-fashioned

One traditional Bulgarian sacrificial ritual features the slaughter and eating of a calf, lamb or fish. The eating can't start before a priest has blessed the meat.

Rodopi mountains

This mountainous area yields mainly potatoes and beans, and it's famous for the quality of its dairy products. Local dishes feature every possible manifestation and transfiguration of the potatoes and some wonderfully strange-looking combinations of ingredients.

Signature dishes (see menu decoder for more dishes)

Пататник	*Patatnik*	Pastry filled with potatoes, cheese, eggs and onion
Клин	*Klin*	Pastry with rice, cheese and herbs
Марудник	*Marudnik*	A type of pancake
Родопско чеверме	*Rodopsko cheverme*	Spit-roast lamb
Смилянски боб	*Smilyanski bob*	Bean salad
Трахана	*Trahana*	Corn, beans and milk
Смидал	*Smidal*	Breadcrumbs with raisins, oil and sugar
Ешлия	*Eshliya*	Sweet fruit soup

Pirin

The most typical dish in this region is meat cooked together with vegetables very slowly: six hours would be a minimum and stewing overnight in a sealed earthenware pot is the norm.

Signature dishes (see menu decoder for more dishes)

Чомлек	*Chomlek*	Beef and potato stew
Капама	*Kapama*	Meat, rice and pickled cabbage stew
Бански старец	*Banski starets*	Dried spicy sausage
Дробка	*Drobka*	Beans with bacon
Цалуварки	*Tsaluvarki*	Beetroot salad
Кървавица	*Karvavitsa*	Spicy pork sausage

Well cheesy!

There is no finer accompaniment to a meal than a blast of *Chalga*, the kitsch, cheesy, alpha-male local folk song. It has to be heard to be believed.

Northern Bulgaria

Nearly every dish from this area includes either eggs, yoghurt or white cheese. A lot of different organic vegetables are grown widely in this mostly lowland area, particularly onion and garlic. An intriguing peculiarity is the use in cooking of nettles, dock leaves and sorrel, as well as many other wild herbs and plants.

Signature dishes (see menu decoder for more dishes)

Лютика	*Lyutika*	Pepper and tomato dip with cheese
Лучник	*Luchnik*	Onion pastry
Панирана коприва	*Panirana kopriva*	Breaded nettle
Еленски бут	*Elenski but*	Spicy dried ham
Пълнен шаран	*Palnen sharan*	Carp stuffed with walnuts and onion

Wine, beer & spirits

Ракия	*Rakiya*	Grape or plum brandy
Мастика	*Mastika*	Aniseed liqueur
Мента	*Menta*	Sweet peppermint liqueur
Пелин	*Pelin*	Bitter wine with herbs
Мавруд	*Mavrud*	Bulgarian red wine
Мелнишко вино	*Melnishko vino*	Bulgarian red wine

Nazdrave

Nazdrave is "cheers" and literally means "to your health". When a toast is proposed, clink your glass with (and make eye contact with) all your companions.

You may hear...

Какво мога да ви предложа?	*Kakvo moga da vi predlozha?*	What can I get you?
Как го искате?	*Kak go iskate?*	How would you like it?
С лед или без лед?	*S led ili bez led?*	With or without ice?
Изстудено или стайна температура?	*Izstudeno ili stayna temperatura?*	Cold or room temperature?

Snacks & refreshments

In large cities breakfast consists of coffee and a cigarette. The coffee served at eateries is espresso and the tea is herbal. The choice for quick street eats is wide – Bulgarian-style pastries, *dyuner* (doner kebabs), various types of toast, slices of pizza and hamburgers.

| Баница | *Banitsa* | Cheese pastry |
| Козунак | *Kozunak* | Sweet bread |

Боза	*Boza*	Sour millet drink
Айран	*Ayran*	Diluted yoghurt drink
Билков чай	*Bilkov chay*	Herbal tea

Vegetarians & special requirements

I'm vegetarian	**Аз съм вегетарианец**	*Az sam vegetarianets*
I don't eat...	**Не ям...**	*Ne yam...*
- meat	**- месо**	*- meso*
- fish	**- риба**	*- riba*
Could you cook something without meat in it?	**Може ли да сготвите нещо без месо?**	*Mozhe li da sgotvite neshto bez meso?*
What's in this?	**Какво има в това?**	*Kakvo ima v tova?*
I'm allergic to...	**Аз съм алергичен към...**	*Az sam alergichen kam...*

Vegetarian options

Although strictly vegetarian restaurants are rare, all eateries offer meat-free meals. When in doubt, ask for *postno yadene* (literally "fasting food"), which is always meat-free.

Children

Are children welcome?	**Децата добре приети ли са тук?**	*Detsata dobre prieti li sa tuk?*
Do you have a children's menu?	**Имате ли детско меню?**	*Imate li detsko menyu?*
What dishes are good for children?	**Кои ястия са подходящи за деца?**	*Koi yastiya sa podhodyashti za detsa?*

Menu decoder

Essentials

Breakfast	Закуска	*Zakuska*
Lunch	Обяд	*Obyad*
Dinner	Вечеря	*Vecherya*
Cover charge	Входна такса/ куверт	*Vhodna taksa/ kuvert*
Vat included	Включено ДДС	*Vklyucheno de de se*
Service included	Включено обслужване	*Vklyucheno obsluzhvane*
Credit cards (not) accepted	Кредитни карти (не) се приемат	*Kreditni karti (ne) se priemat*
First course	Предястие	*Predyastie*
Second course	Основно ястие	*Osnovno yastie*
Dessert	Десерт	*Desert*
Dish of the day	Специалитет на деня	*Spetsialitet na denya*
Local speciality	Местен специалитет	*Mesten spetsialitet*
House specials	Специалитет на заведението	*Spetsialitet na zavedenieto*
A la carte	Меню	*Menyu*
Tourist menu	Туристическо меню	*Turistichesko menyu*
Wine list	Винена листа	*Vinena lista*
Drinks menu	Меню напитки	*Menyu napitki*
Snack menu	Меню закуски	*Menyu zakuski*

Peculiar pizzas

Every town has at least one pizza restaurant, but there's very little that's Italian about the fare: it usually contains local ingredients like *kashkaval* (yellow cheese) instead of parmesan and ham instead of prosciutto.

Munchtime manners
It's polite to wait for the hostess to give the green light before you start eating. Asking for more is regarded as a compliment: go steady to start with so you can manage a second serving.

Methods of preparation

English	Bulgarian	Transliteration
Baked	Печен	*Pechen*
Boiled	Варен	*Varen*
Braised	Задушен	*Zadushen*
Breaded	Паниран	*Paniran*
Deep-fried	Пържен	*Parzhen*
Fresh	Пресен	*Presen*
Fried	Пържен	*Parzhen*
Frozen	Замразен	*Zamrazen*
Grilled/broiled	Печен на скара	*Pechen na skara*
Marinated	Маринован	*Marinovan*
Mashed	Пюре	*Pyure*
Poached	Бланширан	*Blanshiran*
Raw	Суров	*Surov*
Roasted	Печен на фурна	*Pechen na furna*
Salty	Солен	*Solen*
Sautéed	Соте	*Sote*
Smoked	Пушен	*Pushen*
Spicy (flavour)	Ароматен	*Aromaten*
Spicy (hot)	Пикантен	*Pikanten*
Steamed	Парен	*Paren*
Stewed	Задушен	*Zadushen*
Stuffed	Пълнен	*Palnen*
Sweet	Сладък	*Sladak*
Rare	Леко опечен	*Leko opechen*
Medium	Средно опечен	*Sredno opechen*
Well done	Добре опечен	*Dobre opechen*

Common food items

Beef	**Говеждо**	*Govezhdo*
Chicken	**Пилешко**	*Pileshko*
Turkey	**Пуешко**	*Pueshko*
Lamb	**Агнешко**	*Agneshko*
Pork	**Свинско**	*Svinsko*
Fish	**Риба**	*Riba*
Seafood	**Морска храна**	*Morska hrana*
Tuna	**Риба тон**	*Riba ton*
Beans	**Фасул/боб**	*Fasul/bob*
Cheese	**Сирене**	*Sirene*
Eggs	**Яйца**	*Yaytsa*
Lentils	**Леща**	*Leshta*
Pasta/noodles	**Паста/макаронен и изделия**	*Pasta/makaroneni izdeliya*
Rice	**Ориз**	*Oriz*
Aubergine	**Патладжан**	*Patladzhan*
Cabbage	**Зеле**	*Zele*
Carrots	**Моркови**	*Morkovi*
Cucumber	**Краставица**	*Krastavitsa*
Garlic	**Чесън**	*Chesan*
Mushrooms	**Гъби**	*Gabi*
Olives	**Маслини**	*Maslini*
Onion	**Лук**	*Luk*
Potato	**Картоф**	*Kartof*
Red/green pepper	**Червени/зелени чушки**	*Cherveni/zeleni chushki*
Tomato	**Домат**	*Domat*
Vegetables	**Зеленчуци**	*Zelenchutsi*
Bread	**Хляб**	*Hlyab*

Meze
This is an assortment of small dishes served with drinks. It's not an appetiser as such: its purpose is solely to enhance the taste of the drink.

Oil	**Олио**	_Olio_
Pepper	**Пипер**	_Piper_
Salt	**Сол**	_Sol_
Vinegar	**Оцет**	_Otset_
Cake	**Торта**	_Torta_
Cereal	**Зърнена закуска**	_Zarnena zakuska_
Cream	**Крем**	_Krem_
Fruit	**Плод**	_Plod_
Ice cream	**Сладолед**	_Sladoled_
Milk	**Мляко**	_Mlyako_
Tart	**Торта**	_Torta_

Condiments

On your table you will see a bottle of sunflower or olive oil and a bottle of vinegar, plus salt and pepper. You might also find a mixture of salt, red pepper and _chubritsa_ (a native herb) which is used as a dip for bread.

Salads

Шопска салата	_Shopska salata_	Vegetables with white cheese
Овчарска салата	_Ovcharska salata_	_Shopska_ with eggs and mushrooms
Снежанка	_Snezhanka_	Yoghurt with cucumbers, walnuts and garlic
Зелена салата	_Zelena salata_	Lettuce, onion, eggs and radishes
Туршия	_Turshiya_	Pickled vegetables

Soups

Таратор	_Tarator_	Yoghurt, cucumber, dill and garlic soup
Шкембе чорба	_Shkembe chorba_	Tripe soup with garlic
Боб чорба	_Bob chorba_	Spicy bean soup
Курбан чорба	_Kurban chorba_	Spicy lamb soup
Супа топчета	_Supa topcheta_	Meatball soup

Kiselo mlyako

Kiselo mlyako (Bulgarian yoghurt) is unique. It's so thick that when you turn the pot over, it stays where it is. It would make a great face pack.

Starters

Чушка бюрек	*Chushka byurek*	Pepper stuffed with cheese and eggs
Яйца по панагюрски	*Yaytsa po panagyurski*	Poached eggs with yoghurt and garlic
Кашкавал пане	*Kashkaval pane*	Breaded yellow cheese
Тиквички с мляко	*Tikvichki s mlyako*	Courgettes with yoghurt
Сирене по шопски	*Sirene po shopski*	Baked cheese, egg, tomatoes and peppers

Second course dishes

Дроб сърма	*Drob sarma*	Lamb with rice
Гювеч	*Gyuvech*	Spicy meat and vegetable stew
Каварма	*Kavarma*	Meat and vegetable stew
Пълнени чушки	*Palneni chushki*	Stuffed peppers with meat and rice
Сърми	*Sarmi*	Pickled stuffed cabbage leaves
Мусака	*Musaka*	Potatoes, meat and tomatoes
Катино мезе	*Katino meze*	Meat with garlic and mushrooms
Имам баялда	*Imam bayalda*	Stuffed aubergine
Сач	*Sach*	Roasted meat and vegetables
Кюфте	*Kyufte*	Grilled spicy meatball
Кебапче	*Kebapche*	Spicy minced meat, sausage-shaped

Шишче	*Shishche*	Pork kebab
Мешана скара	*Meshana skara*	Mixed grill
Пържола	*Parzhola*	Pork steak

Side dishes

Кьополу	*Kyopolu*	Mashed aubergines, peppers and garlic
Лютеница	*Lyutenitsa*	Mashed peppers, tomatoes and herbs
Катък	*Katak*	Yoghurt with cheese and garlic
Пържени картофи със сирене	*Parzheni kartofi sas sirene*	Chips with white cheese
Сирене	*Sirene*	White brine cheese
Кашкавал	*Kashkaval*	Yellow cheese
Луканка	*Lukanka*	Dried spicy salami-like sausage
Суджук	*Sudzhuk*	Raw dry spicy sausage
Пастърма	*Pastarma*	Spicy beef jerky

Desserts

Тиквена баница	*Tikvena banitsa*	Pumpkin filo pastry
Тулумби	*Tulumbi*	Fried dough lumps in sweet syrup
Торта гараш	*Torta garash*	Chocolate layer cake
Баклава	*Baklava*	Pastry with nuts and sweet syrup
Палачинки	*Palachinki*	Pancakes with various garnishes
Щрудел	*Shtrudel*	Apple pastry
Компот	*Kompot*	Fruit in a sweet syrup
Крем карамел	*Krem caramel*	Caramel custard

Hangover cure
An effective remedy for hangovers is said to be *zeleva chorba* – the juice of pickled sauerkraut. Another possibility is *shkembe chorba* (tripe soup).

Drinks

Ракия	Rakiya	Grape or plum brandy
Червено вино	Cherveno vino	Red wine
Бяло вино	Byalo vino	White wine
Бира	Bira	Beer
Наливна бира	Nalivna bira	Draft beer
Мастика	Mastika	Aniseed liqueur
Мента	Menta	Sweet peppermint liqueur
Пелин	Pelin	Bitter wine with herbs
Айран	Ayran	Diluted yoghurt drink
Боза	Boza	Millet drink
Билков чай	Bilkov chay	Herbal tea

Snacks

Баница	Banitsa	Pastry with cheese and eggs
Козунак	Kozunak	Sweet bread
Мекица	Mekitsa	Deep-fried cakes
Бухти	Buhti	Doughnut-like small cakes
Кифла	Kifla	Dough cakes filled with jam
Поничка	Ponichka	A kind of doughnut
Геврек	Gevrek	A kind of bagel
Принцеса	Printsesa	Grilled meat-and-cheese sandwiches

Rakiya

This local brandy made from different fruits is the national tipple. Most popular are the plum (*slivova*) and grape (*grozdova*) varieties. Its alcohol content is normally around 40 per cent. Rockets have been launched on less.

Shopping

Bulgaria's shopping landscape has been transformed by the advent of upmarket brands and plush, air-conditioned malls that also contain fine restaurants, cosy eateries and modern cinemas. Thankfully, though, visitors can still browse tiny shops, stalls and markets.

Regardless of whether you're bargain-hunting for clothes, cosmetics, accessories or locally made traditional articles, you have a very good chance of finding what you are looking for. The low prices only add to the temptation, so make sure you arrive with plenty of space in your suitcase.

Essentials

Where can I buy...?	Къде мога да купя...?	*Kade moga da kupya...?*
I'd like to buy...	Искам да купя...	*Iskam da kupya...*
Do you have...?	Имате ли...?	*Imate li...?*
Do you sell...?	Продавате ли...?	*Prodavate li...?*
I'd like this	Искам това	*Iskam tova*
I'd prefer...	Предпочитам...	*Predpochitam*
Could you show me...?	Може ли да ми покажете...?	*Mozhe li da mi pokazhete...?*
I'm just looking, thanks	Само разглеждам, благодаря	*Samo razglezhdam, blagodarya*
How much is it?	Колко струва това?	*Kolko struva tova?*
Could you write down the price?	Може ли да ми напишете цената?	*Mozhe li da mi napishete tsenata?*
Do you have any items on sale?	Имате ли разпродажба на някакви стоки?	*Imate li razprodazhba na nyakakvi stoki?*
Could I have a discount?	Може ли да ми направите отстъпка?	*Mozhe li da mi napravite otstapka?*
Nothing else, thanks	Нищо друго, благодаря	*Nishto drugo, blagodarya*
Do you accept credit cards?	Приемате ли кредитни карти?	*Priemate li kreditni karti?*
It's a present: could I have it wrapped, please?	За подарък е, може ли да го опаковате?	*Za podarak e, mozhe li da go opakovate?*

Present and correct

The rule for gift-giving is that it's the thought that counts, not the value. Going over the top runs the risk of embarrassing the recipient, so err on the side of modesty.

Could you post it to...?	Може ли да го изпратите до...?	*Mozhe li da go izpratite do...?*
Can I exchange it?	Може ли да го сменя?	*Mozhe li da go smenya?*
I'd like to return this	Искам да върна това	*Iskam da varna tova*
I'd like a refund	Искам да ми върнете парите	*Iskam da mi varnete parite*

Chiprovtsi kilims

Kilims are hard-wearing, hand-woven rugs that feature the traditional design of brightly coloured triangles and other geometrical shapes. They are entirely made from natural, eco-friendly materials.

Local specialities

Typical local presents or souvenirs are handicraft items such as woodcarvings, rugs in vibrant, pulsating colours and patterns, embroidery and ceramics. The latter are particularly popular, and the distinctive, earth-toned Troyan pottery, which dates back many centuries, is always worth picking up.

The leather and haberdashery industries are big news here, and if you're a fan of the 1970s cop-show look, this is the place to come and seek out that floor-length leather outer garment, not forgetting a chic accessorising whip.

If you're looking for something special for the connoisseur – or for someone who just likes becoming inebriated at top speed – a bottle of *rakiya* (the local grape brandy and national drink) is just the job. Bulgarian wine is always a good idea, especially the unique Melnik and Mavrud varieties, which rival anything you'd find in France. Keen cooks should invest in a pot of the national spice *chubritsa* or maybe a hunk of local cheese, especially the white brine *sirene*, whose slightly gritty texture makes it fascinating to cook with.

Religious icons are widely available and range from the camp and kitsch to the absolutely stunning. Much the same can be said of the various souvenirs you can buy from Communist times. However, do be careful not to fall prey to purveyors of realistic fakes.

Can you recommend a shop selling local specialities?	Можете ли да ми препоръчате магазин за местни сувенири?	_Mozhete li da mi preporachate magazin za mestni suveniri?_
What are the local specialities?	Кои са традиционните специалитети?	_Koi sa tradizionnite spezialiteti?_
What should I buy from here?	Какво трябва да си купя от тук?	_Kakvo tryabva da si kupya ot tuk?_
Is this good quality?	Това качествено ли е?	_Tova kachestveno li e?_
Do you make this yourself?	Вие сам ли го правите?	_Vie sam li go pravite?_
Is it handmade?	Това ръчна изработка ли е?	_Tova rachna izrabotka li e?_
Do you make it to measure?	Правите ли го по мярка?	_Pravite li go po myarka?_
Can I order one?	Може ли да поръчам един/ една/едно?	_Mozhe li da poracham edin/ edna/edno?_

Popular things to buy

Дърворезба	_Darvorezba_	Woodcarvings
Икони	_Ikoni_	Orthodox icons

Rose oil

Some 60,000 roses are needed to distil a single ounce of oil – that's about 60 per drop. The flower is said to contain properties that heal emotional wounds.

Керамика	Keramika	Traditionally painted ceramics
Бродерия	Broderiya	Embroidered clothing and tablecloths
Килими	Kilimi	Handwoven woollen carpets and rugs
Ракия	Rakiya	Grape or plum brandy
Червено вино	Cherveno vino	Red wine
Сирене	Sirene	White brine cheese
Чубрица	Chubritsa	Local herb
Розово масло	Rozovo maslo	Rose oil and its products
Медни съдове	Medni sadove	Handmade coppery utensils
Чанове	Chanove	Cow bells
Сребърна бижутерия	Srebarna bizhuteriya	Ethnic silver jewellery
Пчелен мед	Pchelen med	Honey in various flavours

Assistants with attitude

Many Bulgarian clothes shop assistants look like supermodels and have an attitude to match. Being treated like an insignificant nuisance by them is all part of the experience.

Clothes & shoes

Those temples of the glorious new world of Capitalism, the shopping malls that line Bulgaria's increasingly consumer-clogged streets, are full and, unlike in the old days, certainly offer the customer choice. However, that choice is limited to mainstream international labels; and the genuine luxury brand goods that you can now buy here cost pretty much the same as in other countries. Why, you might well ask, should anyone bother to shop for togs and footwear here at all? The answer is that you can score big time if you eschew the well-known brands. Bulgaria certainly isn't the place to get your credit limit raised for if you want familiar and mass-produced anything: you'd be better off staying at home. This country is now all about individuality and quirkiness. Thus you will find that locally produced clothing and footwear is significantly cheaper, more chic and most definitely funkier than almost anything you find in Blighty.

Where is the... department?	Къде е секторът за...?	Kade e sektorat za...?
- clothes	- дрехи	- drehi
- shoe	- обувки	- obuvki
- women's	- жени	- zheni
- men's	- мъже	- mazhe
- children's	- деца	- detsa

Which floor is the...?	На кой етаж е...?	Na koy etazh e...?

I'm looking for...	Търся...	Tarsya...
- a skirt	- пола	- pola
- trousers	- панталони	- pantaloni
- a top	- блуза	- bluza
- a jacket	- яке	- yake
- a T-shirt	- тениска	- teniska
- jeans	- джинси	- dzhinsi
- shoes	- обувки	- obuvki
- underwear	- бельо	- belyo

Can I try it on?	Може ли да го пробвам?	Mozhe li da go probvam?

Only as a last resort
Don't shop for local specialities in resorts – these tourist traps offer kitsch, hopelessly outdated examples at inflated prices. Good quality items and genuine traditional bargains can be bought from artisans' workshops.

Klek shops
These shifty shops sell cut-price cigarettes, cheap booze, flat soft drinks and out-of-date food. Very interesting in socio-economic terms, but file under "Avoid".

What size is it?	**Какъв размер е?**	*Kakav razmer e?*
My size is...	**Моят размер е...**	*Moyat razmer e...*
- small	**- S**	*- es*
- medium	**- M**	*- em*
- large	**- L**	*- el*

(see clothes size converter on p96 for full range of sizes)

Do you have this in my size?	**Имате ли моя размер?**	*Imate li moya razmer ot tova?*
Where is the changing room?	**Къде е пробната?**	*Kade e probnata?*

It doesn't fit	**Не ми става**	*Ne mi stava*
It doesn't suit me	**Не ми стои добре**	*Ne mi stoi dobre*
Do you have a... size?	**Имате ли... размер?**	*Imate li... razmer?*
- bigger	**- по-голям**	*- po-golyam*
- smaller	**- по-малък**	*- po-malak*

Do you have it/ them in...	**Имате ли го/ ги в...**	*Imate li go/ gi v...*
- black?	**- черно?**	*- cherno?*
- white?	**- бяло?**	*- byalo?*
- blue?	**- синьо?**	*- sinyo?*
- green?	**- зелено?**	*- zeleno?*
- red?	**- червено?**	*- cherveno?*

Are they made of leather?	**Кожени ли са?**	*Kozheni li sa?*
I'm going to leave it/them	**Ще го/ги оставя**	*Shte go/gi ostavya*
I'll take it/them	**Ще го/ги взема**	*Shte go/gi vzema*

You may hear...

Мога ли да ви помогна?	*Moga li da vi pomogna?*	Can I help you?
Обслужиха ли ви?	*Obsluzhiha li vi?*	Have you been served?
Какъв размер?	*Kakav razmer?*	What size?
Нямаме	*Nyamame*	We don't have any
Заповядайте	*Zapovyadayte*	Here you are
Нещо друго?	*Neshto drugo?*	Anything else?
Да ви го опаковам ли?	*Da vi go opakovam li?*	Shall I wrap it for you?
Това е (50) лева	*Tova e (50) leva*	It's (50) leva
Това е намалено	*Tova e namaleno*	It's reduced

Mente

This word, meaning "cheap imitation", can be applied to dodgy goods... and dodgy characters, too (especially politicians).

Where to shop

Where can I find a...	Къде мога да намеря...	*Kade moga da namerya...*
- bookshop?	- книжарница?	- *knizharnitsa?*
- clothes shop?	- магазин за дрехи?	- *magazin za drehi?*
- department store?	- универсален магазин?	- *universalen magazin?*
- gift shop?	- магазин за подаръци?	- *magazin za podaratsi?*
- music shop?	- музикален магазин?	- *muzikalen magazin?*
- market?	- пазар?	- *pazar?*
- newsagent?	- магазин за вестници и списания?	- *magazin za vestnitsi i spisaniya?*
- shoe shop?	- магазин за обувки?	- *magazin za obuvki?*

- stationer's?	- **магазин за канцеларски материали?**	- *magazin za kantselarski materiali?*
- tobacconist?	- **магазин за тютюневи изделия?**	- *magazin za tyutyunevi izdeliya?*
- souvenir shop?	- **магазин за сувенири?**	- *magazin za suveniri?*
Where's the best place to buy...?	**Къде е най-доброто място да купя...?**	*Kade e nay-dobroto myasto da kupya?*
- a film	- **лента за фотоапарат**	- *lenta za fotoaparat*
- an English newspaper	- **английски вестник**	- *angliyski vestnik*
- a map	- **карта**	- *karta*
- postcards	- **пощенски картички**	- *poshtenski kartichki*
- a present	- **подарък**	- *podarak*
- stamps	- **марки**	- *marki*
- sun cream	- **слънцезащитен крем**	- *slantsezashtiten krem*

For that Socialist souvenir…
If you find yourself getting all nostalgic for Iron-Curtain times, Sofia's open-air antique market, with its authentic medals, military items and statuettes, will be right up your politburo.

Food & markets

Is there a supermarket/ market nearby?	**Има ли супермаркет/ пазар наблизо?**	*Ima li supermarket/ pazar nablizo?*

Can I have...	Може ли...	*Mozhe li...*
- some bread?	- малко хляб?	*- malko hlyab?*
- some fruit?	- малко плодове?	*- malko plodove?*
- some cheese?	- малко сирене?	*- malko sirene?*
- a bottle of water?	- бутилка вода?	*- butilka voda?*
- a bottle of wine?	- бутилка вино?	*- butilka vino?*

I'd like... of that	Искам... от това	*Iskam... ot tova*
- half a kilo	- половин килограм	*- polovin kilogram*
- 250 grams	- 250 грама	*- 250 grama*
- a small/big piece	- малко/голямо парче	*- malko/golyamo parche*

Import & export

The maximum limit for both the import and export of drinks is 11 litres of spirits and 21 litres of wine. Jewellery and accessories containing up to 60 grammes of gold and platinum, or up to 300 grammes of silver, need not be declared. You are not allowed to export antiques, artworks and valuable collectable coins unless you have a permit issued by the Ministry of Culture.

Retail revolution!

Capitalism – or maybe perhaps just shopping – has proved to be so seductive to Bulgarians that in 2008 the city of Varna announced plans to build Bulgaria's biggest mall, the 145,000 sq metre Park Cherno More. So much for Communism, then (that whirring sound is Karl Marx going Dervish in his grave).

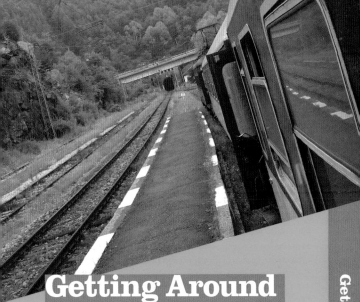

Getting Around

Travelling by bus is the quickest and best way to get around Bulgaria. That said, the buses that serve rural areas aren't always as swish as the ones that operate in towns and cities.

Train travel is cheaper, but intercity and express services only operate on the main routes. Any other rail experiences can involve a lot of waiting around and the honing of survival skills. On the plus side, you will get a great view of the countryside and have a very sociable journey – you will end up talking to your fellow passengers one way or the other.

If you decide to travel by car, don't expect to get anywhere quickly. Or cheaply. Or calmly.

Arrival

At the international airports in Sofia, Varna and Burgas you'll find the usual ATMs, car hire counters and travel agencies, but eating and shopping facilities will be limited. Remember that if you are not an EU citizen and are not staying at a hotel, you have to register with the local police. Otherwise you might be fined when leaving the country.

Where is/are the...	Къде е/са...	Kade e/sa...
- luggage from flight...?	- багажът от полет...?	- bagazhat ot polet...?
- luggage trolleys?	- количките за багаж?	- kolichkite za bagazh?
- lost luggage office?	- бюрото за загубен багаж?	- byuroto za zaguben bagazh?

Where is/are the...	Къде е/са...	Kade e/sa...
- buses?	- автобусите?	- avtobusite?
- trains?	- влаковете?	- vlakovete?
- taxis?	- такситата?	- taksitata?
- car rental?	- колите под наем?	- kolite pod naem?
- exit?	- изходът?	- izhodat?

How do I get to hotel...?	Как да стигна до хотел..?	Kak da stigna do hotel...?

My baggage is...	Моят багаж е...	Moyat bagazh e...
- lost	- изгубен	- izguben
- damaged	- повреден	- povreden
- stolen	- откраднат	- otkradnat

Backpacking

Inexplicably, Bulgaria is not (yet) very popular as a backpackers' destination, although it is absolutely possible to travel around the country on a budget. Bulgarians do it all the time!

Customs

Bulgaria's customs regulations are the same as those of other EU countries. Additionally, for the export of some antiques and artworks you need a special permit from the Ministry of Culture. Due to fears about child trafficking, the authorities are particularly strict – travellers with children may be asked for documents to prove their parental relationship.

The children are on this passport	**Децата са на този паспорт**	*Detsata sa na tozi passport*
We're here on holiday	**Ние сме на почивка**	*Nie sme na pochivka*
I'm going to...	**Отивам до...**	*Otivam do...*
I have nothing to declare	**Нямам нищо за деклариране**	*Nyamam nishto za deklarirane*
Do I have to declare this?	**Трябва ли да декларирам това?**	*Tryabva li da deklariram tova?*

Car hire

All the international brand car hire companies have offices at the airport and in Sofia city centre, as well as outlets in the bigger hotels. There are also many reliable local companies offering considerably cheaper rates. It's a good idea to make an online booking in advance.

I'd like to hire a...	**Искам да наема...**	*Iskam da naema...*
- car	**- кола**	*- kola*
- people carrier	**- пътнически ван**	*- patnicheski van*
with...	**с...**	*s...*
- air conditioning	**- климатик**	*- klimatik*
- automatic transmission	**- автоматични скорости**	*- avtomatichni skorosti*
How much is that for a...	**Колко струва на...**	*Kolko struva na...*
- day?	**- ден?**	*- den?*
- week?	**- седмица?**	*- sedmitsa?*
Does that include...	**Това включва ли...**	*Tova vklyuchva li...*
- mileage?	**- километраж?**	*- kilometrazh?*
- insurance?	**- застраховка?**	*- zastrahovka?*

On the road

A road trip through the country can be quite a challenge. Many of the secondary roads are in pretty bad condition, and the majority of road signs are in Cyrillic only, so it's good to have a bilingual map. Don't forget that most Bulgarian drivers feel that road rules are for unimaginative wimps.

What is the speed limit?	Какво е ограничението за скорост?	*Kakvo e ogranichenieto za skorost?*
Can I park here?	Може ли да паркирам тук?	*Mozhe li da parkiram tuk?*
Where is a petrol station?	Къде има бензиностанция?	*Kade ima benzinostantsiya?*
Please fill up the tank with...	Моля, напълнете резервоара с...	*Molya, napalnete rezervoara s...*
- unleaded	- безоловен	*- bezoloven*
- diesel	- дизел	*- dizel*
- leaded	- оловен	*- oloven*
- LPG	- газ	*- gaz*

Donkey carts

In Bulgaria, the old and the new coexist in harmony. Expensive shiny modern cars share the road with horse or donkey carts – an ecological and fuel-saving means of transport.

Directions

Is this the road to...?	Това ли е пътят за...?	*Tova li e patyat za...?*
How do I get to...?	Как да стигна до...?	*Kak da stigna do...?*
How far is it to...?	Колко далече е до...?	*Kolko daleche e do...?*
How long will it take to...?	Колко време ще отнеме до...?	*Kolko vreme shte otneme do...?*
Could you point it out on the map?	Може ли да го покажете на картата?	*Mozhe li da go pokazhete na kartata?*

I've lost my way	**Загубих пътя**	_Zagubih patya_
On the right/left	**Отдясно/отляво**	_Otdyasno/otlyavo_
Turn right/left	**Завийте надясно/**	_Zaviyte nadyasno/_
	наляво	_nalyavo_
Straight ahead	**Направо**	_Napravo_
Turn around	**Обърнете обратно**	_Obarnete obratno_

Public transport

Public transport is relatively inexpensive but generally slow and scruffy, especially the trains. Coaches, especially those on main routes, are new, modern, regular and pretty fast, so they're the best option for certain destinations. There are daily flights from Sofia to coastal resort towns, but they can work out up to five times more expensive than road or rail options.

Bus	**Автобус**	_Avtobus_
Bus station	**Автогара**	_Avtogara_
Train	**Влак**	_Vlak_
Train station	**ЖП гара**	_Zhe pe gara_
I would like to go to...	**Искам да отида до...**	_Iskam da otida do..._
I would like a... ticket	**Искам... билет**	_Iskam... bilet_
- single	**- еднопосочен**	_- ednoposochen_
- return	**- за отиване и връщане**	_- za otivane i vrashtane_
- first class	**- първа класа**	_- parva klasa_
- smoking/ non-smoking	**- за пушачи/ за непушачи**	_- za pushachi/ za nepushachi_
What time does it leave/arrive?	**В колко часа тръгва/пристига?**	_V kolko chasa tragva/pristiga?_
Could you tell me when to get off?	**Можете ли да ми кажете къде да сляза?**	_Mozhete li da mi kazhete kade da slyaza?_

Taxis

To avoid being ripped off, it's best to stick to legitimate taxi companies and avoid the plucky freelancers. Even in licensed cabs, it's better to agree a fee before you set off, rather than rely on a meter. Taxi drivers rarely speak foreign languages and are often grumpy and impolite. Have a nice day!

I'd like a taxi to...	Искам такси до...	*Iskam taksi do...*
How much is it to the...	Колко струва до...	*Kolko struva do...*
- airport?	- летището?	*- letishteto?*
- town centre?	- центъра на града?	*- tsentara na grada?*
- hotel?	- хотела?	*- hotela?*

Tours

Bulgaria is well known for its seaside and ski resorts. The country's magnificent mountains provide hundreds of hiking trails, unlimited opportunities for climbing and serious caving possibilities. Via Pontica Bulgaria, which is on a major bird migration route, is a renowned destination for bird watching.

Are there any organised tours of the town/region?	Има ли някакви организирани обиколки на града/региона?	*Ima li nyakakvi organizirani obikolki na grada/regiona?*
Where do they leave from?	От къде тръгват?	*Otkade tragvat?*
What time does it start?	Кога започва?	*Koga zapochva?*
Do you have English-speaking guides?	Имате ли екскурзоводи на английски?	*Imate li ekskurzovodi na angliyski?*
Is lunch/tea included?	Включен ли е обяд/чай?	*Vklyuchen li e obyad/chay?*
Do we get any free time?	Имаме ли някакво свободно време?	*Imame li nyakakvo svobodno vreme?*
Are we going to see...?	Ще видим ли...?	*Shte vidim li...?*
What time do we get back?	Кога ще се върнем?	*Koga shte se varnem?*

Fast resorts

Unfortunately, the race to attract tourists has led to rushed construction projects that give no thought to infrastructure or green spaces. Some tourists still find themselves holidaying on a building site.

Accommodation

Accommodation

Bulgaria offers a wide choice of
accommodation. In terms of hotels,
you can find everything from luxury
5-star chains through to smaller,
comfortable 3-star places. There are an
increasing number of good hostels,
serviced apartments and very cheap
private rooms.

Hotels are no longer allowed to operate
the two-tier system that used to charge
foreigners considerably higher prices.
Most hoteliers list their prices in euros
but you can pay the equivalent rate in
the local currency, *leva*, if you wish.
Although there is no shortage of
accommodation, advance booking is
advisable especially if you're travelling
to major resorts in high season.

Types of accommodation

Officially hotels are classified according to the European star-grading system. In most cases the rating is a reasonably accurate reflection of reality, but the quality of facilities and services is not always up to the advertised standard. In the smaller resorts and villages you can find cheap private rooms by asking around. These are often in atmospheric, traditional houses whose amenities are basic but functional.

I'd like to stay in...	Искам да отседна в...	Iskam da otsedna v...
- an apartment	- апартамент	- apartment
- a campsite	- къмпинг	- kamping
- a hotel	- хотел	- hotel
- a serviced room	- обслужвана стая	- obsluzhvana staya
- a youth hostel	- хостел	- hostel
- a guest house	- къща за гости	- kashta za gosti

Is it...	Това... ли е?	Tova... li e?
- full board?	- пълен пасион	- palen pansion
- half board?	- полу-пансион	- polu-pansion
- self-catering?	- без храна	- bez hrana

Monasteries

The accommodation offered by Bulgarian monasteries may not be up to boutique hotel levels of luxury, but these centuries-old religious sanctuaries provide a uniquely beautiful experience.

Reservations

Do you have any rooms available?	Имате ли свободни стаи?	Imate li svobodni stai?
Can you recommend anywhere else?	Можете ли да ми препоръчате някъде другаде?	Mozhete li da mi preporachate nyakade drugade?
I'd like to make a reservation for...	Искам да направя резервация за...	Iskam da napravya rezervaziya za...

- tonight	**- довечера**	- dovechera
- one night	**- една нощ**	- edna nosht
- two nights	**- две нощи**	- dve noshti
- a week	**- една седмица**	- edna sedmitsa

From... (1st May)	**От ...(първи май)**	Ot... (parvi may)
to... (8th May)	**до...(осми май)**	do... (osmi may)

Mountain huts

Those who love to go a-wandering will come across *hizha* (mountain huts). Their rooms are a touch primitive, but they never turn anyone away, even if it's standing room only.

Room types

Air conditioning, cable or satellite TV, mini-bar and Internet access are standard features in 3-star hotel rooms and above. Some have full size baths, some only showers; if access to one or the other is important for you, ask in advance. Don't expect to find kettles in most cases, though in apartments you can expect a fully equipped kitchen.

Do you have... room?	**Имате ли... стая?**	Imate li... staya?
- a single	**- единична**	- edinichna
- a double	**- двойна**	- dvoyna
- a family	**- семейна**	- semeyna

with...	**с...**	s...
- a cot?	**- детско легло?**	- detsko leglo?
- twin beds?	**- две отделни легла?**	- dve otdelni legla?
- a double bed?	**- двойно легло?**	- dvoyno leglo?
- a bath/shower?	**- баня/душ?**	- banya/dush?
- air conditioning?	**- климатик?**	- klimatik?
- Internet access?	**- интернет връзка?**	- internet vrazka?

Can I see the room?	**Може ли да видя стаята?**	Mozhe li da vidya stayata?

Spa hotels
Bulgaria ranks among the top locations in Europe for mineral-rich water and healing mud. Hence the plethora of spa hotels offering treatments and healing therapies.

Prices

Bulgarian accommodation prices are lower than in most other European countries, especially outside Sofia and other popular resorts. Most hotels offer discounted weekend rates. Breakfast is usually included in the price, as is Internet access, but do check before you book. As in the rest of the world, phone calls and mini-bar goodies are overpriced.

How much is...	Колко струва...	*Kolko struva...*
- a double room?	- двойна стая?	*- dvoyna staya?*
- per night?	- на нощ?	*- na nosht?*
- per week?	- на седмица?	*- na sedmitsa?*
Is breakfast included?	Включена ли е закуска?	*Vklyuchena li e zakuska?*
Do you have...	Имате ли...	*Imate li...*
- a reduction for children?	- намаление за деца?	*- namalenie za detsa?*
- a single room supplement?	- допълнително легло към единична стая?	*- dopalnitelno leglo kam edinichna staya?*
Is there...	Има ли...	*Ima li...*
- a swimming pool?	- плувен басейн?	*- pluven baseyn?*
- a lift?	- асансьор?	*- asansyor?*
I'll take it	Ще я взема	*Shte ya vzema*
Can I pay by...	Мога ли да платя с...	*Moga li da platya s...*
- credit card?	- кредитна карта?	*- kreditna karta?*
- traveller's cheque?	- пътнически чек?	*- patnicheski chek?*

Special requests

Could you...	Може ли...	Mozhe li...
- put this in the hotel safe?	- да сложите това в сейфа на хотела?	- da slozhite tova v seyfa na hotela?
- order a taxi for me?	- да ми поръчате такси?	- da mi porachate taksi?
- wake me up at 7am?	- да ме събудите в 7 часа сутринта?	- da me sabudite v sedem chasa sutrinta?

Can I have...	Може ли да ми дадете...	Mozhe li da mi dadete...
- a room with a sea view?	- стая с изглед към морето?	- staya s izgled kam moreto?
- a bigger room?	- по-голяма стая?	- po-golyama staya?
- a quieter room?	- по-тиха стая?	- po-tiha staya?

Is there...	Има ли...	Ima li...
- a safe?	- сейф?	- seyf?
- a babysitting service?	- услуга гледане на деца?	- usluga gledane na detsa?
- a laundry service?	- пералня?	- peralnya?

24/7 pit stops
If you arrive earlier than intended or with no accommodation arranged you'll be pleased to find one of the many new 24/7 venues, designed to provide refreshment and a pew for the weary traveller.

| Is there wheelchair access? | Има ли достъп за инвалидни колички? | *Ima li dostap za invalidni kolichki?* |

Checking in & out

I have a reservation for tonight	Имам резервация за тази вечер	*Imam rezervatsiya za tazi vecher*
In the name of...	На името на...	*Na imeto na...*
Here's my passport	Заповядайте, моя паспорт	*Zapovyadayte, moya passport*
What time is check out?	Кога трябва да освободя стаята?	*Koga tryabva da osvobodya stayata?*
Can I have a later check out?	Може ли да я освободя по-късно?	*Mozhe li da ya osvobodya po-kasno?*
Can I leave my bags here?	Може ли да си оставя чантите тук?	*Mozhe li da si ostavya chantite tuk?*
I'd like to check out	Искам да освободя стаята	*Iskam da osvobodya stayata*
Can I have the bill?	Може ли сметката?	*Mozhe li smetkata?*

Camping

Do you have...	Имате ли...	*Imate li...*
- a site available?	- свободно място?	*- svobodno myasto?*
- electricity?	- електричество?	*- elektrichestvo?*
- hot showers?	- душове с топла вода?	*- dushove s topla voda?*
- tents for hire?	- палатки под наем?	*- palatki pod naem?*

How much is it per...	Колко струва на...	*Kolko struva na...*
- tent?	- палатка?	*- palatka?*
- caravan?	- каравана?	*- karavana?*
- person?	- човек?	*- chovek?*
- car?	- кола?	*- kola?*

Where is/are the...	Къде е/са...	*Kade e/sa...*
- reception?	- рецепцията?	*- retseptsiyata?*
- bathrooms?	- баните?	*- banite?*
- laundry facilities?	- пералното помещение?	*- peralnoto pomeshtenie?*

Survival Guide

Metered cabins in post offices or public phones (cards are available from news stands and kiosks) provide a cheaper alternative to hotel room calls. All local mobile operators offer prepaid cards and there are internet cafés in every town. Money can be changed at banks or at bureaux de change. Anyone offering to exchange money on the street will be dodgy.

Minor ailments can be dealt with in a pharmacy, which are plentiful (though staff rarely speak English, so take this guide with you). In summer you'll need sunscreen and an insect repellent. Tap water is safe to drink, though mineral water is freely available.

Money & banks

Where is the nearest...	Къде е...	Kade e...
- bank?	- най-близката банка?	- nay-blizkata banka?
- ATM?	- най-близкият банкомат?	- nay-blizkiyat bankomat?
- foreign exchange office?	- най-близкото обменно бюро?	- nay-blizkoto obmenno byuro?
I'd like to...	Искам...	Iskam...
- withdraw money	- да изтегля пари	- da izteglya pari
- cash a traveller's cheque	- да осребря пътнически чек	- da osrebrya patnicheski chek
- change money	- да обменя пари	- da obmenya pari
- arrange a transfer	- да направя паричен превод	- da napravya parichen prevod
Could I have smaller notes, please?	Може ли по-дребни банкноти, моля?	Mozhe li po-drebni banknoti, molya?
What's the exchange rate?	Какъв е обменният курс?	Kakav e obmenniyat kurs?
What's the commission?	Каква е комисионата?	Kakva e komisionata?
What's the charge for...	Каква е таксата за...	Kakva e taksata za...
- making a withdrawal?	- изтегляне на пари?	- izteglyane na pari?
- exchanging money?	- обмяна на пари?	- obmyana na pari?
- cashing a cheque?	- осребряване на чек?	- osrebryavane na chek?
What's the minimum/ maximum amount?	Каква е минималната/ максималната сума?	Kakva e minimalnata/ maksimalnata suma?
This is not right	Това не е вярно	Tova ne e vyarno
Is there a problem with my account?	Проблем ли има с моята сметка?	Problem li ima s moyata smetka?
The ATM took my card	Банкоматът ми глътна картата	Bankomat mi glatna kartata
I've forgotten my PIN	Забравил съм си PIN-кода	Zabravil sam si PIN-koda

The number is...	Номерът е...	*Nomerat e...*
What's the area/country code for...?	Какъв е селищният/ международният телефонен код за...?	*Kakav e selishtniyat/ mezhdunarodniyat telefonen kod za...?*
The number is engaged	Номерът дава заето	*Nomerat dava zaeto*
The connection is bad	Връзката е лоша	*Vrazkata e losha*
I've been cut off	Връзката прекъсна	*Vrazkata prekasna*
I'd like...	Искам...	*Iskam...*
- a charger for my mobile phone	- зарядно за моя мобилен телефон	*- zaryadno za moya mobilen telefon*
- an adaptor plug	- адаптор	*- adaptor*
- a pre-paid SIM card	- предплатена СИМ карта	*- predplatena SIM karta*

Internet

Where's the nearest Internet café?	Къде е най- близкият интернет клуб?	*Kade e nay-blizkiyat internet klub?*
Can I access the Internet here?	Има ли интернет връзка тук?	*Ima li internet vrazka tuk?*
I'd like to...	Искам...	*Iskam...*
- use the Internet	- да ползвам интернет	*- da polzvam internet*
- check my email	- да си проверя пощата	*- da si proverya poshtata*
- use a printer	- да ползвам принтер	*- da polzvam printer*
How much is it...	Колко струва...	*Kolko struva...*
- per minute?	- на минута?	*- na minuta?*
- per hour?	- на час?	*- na chas?*
- to buy a CD?	- да купя CD?	*- da kupya si di?*
How do I...	Как да...	*Kak da...*
- log on?	- вляза?	*- vlyaza?*
- open a browser?	- отворя браузър?	*- da otvorya brauzar?*
- print this?	- принтирам/ разпечатам това?	*- da printiram/ razpechatam tova?*

The number is...	Номерът е...	*Nomerat e...*
What's the area/country code for...?	Какъв е селищният/ международният телефонен код за...?	*Kakav e selishtniyat/ mezhdunarodniyat telefonen kod za...?*
The number is engaged	Номерът дава заето	*Nomerat dava zaeto*
The connection is bad	Връзката е лоша	*Vrazkata e losha*
I've been cut off	Връзката прекъсна	*Vrazkata prekasna*
I'd like...	Искам...	*Iskam...*
- a charger for my mobile phone	- зарядно за моя мобилен телефон	*- zaryadno za moya mobilen telefon*
- an adaptor plug	- адаптор	*- adaptor*
- a pre-paid SIM card	- предплатена СИМ карта	*- predplatena SIM karta*

Internet

Where's the nearest Internet café?	Къде е най- близкият интернет клуб?	*Kade e nay-blizkiyat internet klub?*
Can I access the Internet here?	Има ли интернет връзка тук?	*Ima li internet vrazka tuk?*
I'd like to...	Искам...	*Iskam...*
- use the Internet	- да ползвам интернет	*- da polzvam internet*
- check my email	- да си проверя пощата	*- da si proverya poshtata*
- use a printer	- да ползвам принтер	*- da polzvam printer*
How much is it...	Колко струва...	*Kolko struva...*
- per minute?	- на минута?	*- na minuta?*
- per hour?	- на час?	*- na chas?*
- to buy a CD?	- да купя CD?	*- da kupya si di?*
How do I...	Как да...	*Kak da...*
- log on?	- вляза?	*- vlyaza?*
- open a browser?	- отворя браузър?	*- da otvorya brauzar?*
- print this?	- принтирам/ разпечатам това?	*- da printiram/ razpechatam tova?*

I need help with this computer	Имам нужда от помощ с този компютър	Imam nuzhda ot pomosht s tozi kompyutar
The computer has crashed	Компютърът се развали	Kompyutarat se razvali
I've finished	Аз свърших	Az svarshih

Chemist

Where's the nearest (all-night) pharmacy?	Къде е най-близката (денонощна) аптека?	Kade e nay-blizkata (denonoshtna) apteka?
What time does the pharmacy open/close?	Кога отваря/затваря аптеката?	Koga otvarya/zatvarya aptekata?
I need something for...	Нуждая се от нещо за...	Nuzhdaya se ot neshto za...
- diarrhoea	- диария	- diariya
- a cold	- простуда	- prostuda
- a cough	- кашлица	- kashlitsa
- insect bites	- ухапване от насекоми	- uhapvane ot nasekomi
- sunburn	- слънчево изгаряне	- slanchevo izgaryane
- motion sickness	- световъртеж	- svetovartezh
- hay fever	- сенна хрема	- senna hrema
- period pain	- менструални болки	- menstrualni bolki
- abdominal pains	- коремни болки	- koremni bolki
- a urine infection	- инфекция на пикочните пътища	- infektsiya na pikochnite patishta
- a vaginal infection	- вагинална инфекция	- vaginalna infektsiya

Herbal healing

Bulgarian herbal pharmacists are outstandingly competent, providing conventional medicines alongside advice on herbal options.

I'd like...	Искам…	_Iskam..._
- aspirin	- аспирин	- _aspirin_
- plasters	- пластир	- _plastir_
- condoms	- презервативи	- _prezervativi_
- insect repellent	- репелент	- _repellent_
- painkillers	- обезболяващи	- _obezbolyavashti_
- a contraceptive	- противозачатъчни	- _protivozachatachni_

How much should I take?	Колко трябва да взема?	_Kolko tryabva da vzema?_
Take...	Вземете…	_Vzemete..._
- a tablet	- една таблетка	- _edna tabletka_
- a teaspoon	- чаена лъжичка	- _chaena lazhichka_
- with water	- с вода	- _s voda_

How often should I take this?	Колко често трябва да вземам това?	_Kolko chesto tryabva da vzemam tova?_
- once/twice a day	- веднъж/два пъти на ден	- _vednazh/dva pati na den_
- before/after meals	- преди/след ядене	- _predi/sled yadene_
- in the morning/ evening	- сутрин/вечер	- _sutrin/vecher_

Is it suitable for children?	Подходящо ли е за деца?	_Podhodyashto li e za detsa?_
Will it make me drowsy?	Ще ме направи ли сънлив?	_Shte me napravi li sanliv?_
Do I need a prescription?	Нуждая ли се от рецепта?	_Nuzhdaya li se ot retsepta?_
I have a prescription	Имам рецепта	_Imam retsepta_

Bin there, seen it, dumped it

Categorised rubbish collection for recycling is uncommon in Bulgaria. Coloured bins are purely for aesthetic reasons, and any bin is fair game for your rubbish.

Children

Where should I take the children?	Къде да заведа децата?	Kade da zaveda detsata?
Where is...	Къде е…	Kade e...
- the nearest playground?	- най-близката детска площадка?	- nay-blizkata detska ploshadka?
- the nearest fairground?	- най-близкият увеселителен парк?	- nay-blizkiyat uveselitelen park?
- the nearest zoo?	- най-близката зоологическа градина?	- nay-blizkata zoologicheska gradina?
- the nearest park?	- най-близкият парк?	- nay-blizkiyat park?
- the nearest swimming pool?	- най-близкият плувен басейн?	- nay-blizkiyat pluven baseyn?
Is this suitable for children?	Това подходящо ли е за деца?	Tova podhodyashto li e za detsa?
Are children allowed?	Разрешено ли е за деца?	Razresheno li e za detsa?
Are there baby-changing facilities here?	Има ли стая за майки с малки деца?	Ima li staya za mayki s malki detsa?
Do you have...	Имате ли…	Imate li...
- a children's menu?	- детско меню?	- detsko menyu?
- a high chair?	- детско столче?	- detsko stolche?
Is there...	Има ли…	Ima li...
- a child-minding service?	- услуга гледане на деца?	- usluga gledane na detsa?
- a nursery?	- детска ясла?	- detska yasla?
Can you recommend a reliable babysitter?	Може ли да ми препоръчате добра детегледачка?	Mozhe li da mi preporachate dobra detegledachka?
Are the children constantly supervised?	Децата непрекъснато ли се наглеждат?	Detsata neprekasnato li se naglezhdat?
When can I bring them?	Кога мога да ги доведа?	Koga moga da gi doveda?

What time do I have to pick them up?	Кога трябва да ги взема?	*Koga tryabva da gi vzema?*
He/she is... years old	Той/тя е на… години	*Toy/tya e na... godini*
I'd like to buy...	Искам да купя…	*Iskam da kupya...*
- nappies	- пеленки	*- pelenki*
- baby wipes	- бебешки мокри кърпички	*- bebeshki mokri karpichki*
- tissues	- кърпички	*- karpichki*

Travellers with disabilities

I have a disability	Аз имам увреждане	*Az imam uvrezhdane*
I need assistance	Имам нужда от помощ	*Imam nuzhda ot pomosht*
I am blind	Аз съм сляп	*Az sam slyap*
I am deaf	Аз съм глух	*Az sam gluh*
I have a hearing aid	Имам слухов апарат	*Imam sluhov aparat*
I can't walk well	Не мога да ходя добре	*Ne moga da hodya dobre*
Is there a lift?	Има ли асансьор?	*Ima li asansyor?*
Is there wheelchair access?	Има ли достъп за инвалидни колички?	*Ima li dostap za invalidni kolichki?*
Can I bring my guide dog?	Може ли да доведа моето куче водач?	*Mozhe li da doveda moeto kuche vodach?*
Are there disabled toilets?	Има ли тоалетни за инвалиди?	*Ima li toaletni za invalidi?*
Do you offer disabled assistance?	Предлагате ли обслужване за инвалиди?	*Predlagate li obsluzhvane za invalidi?*
Could you help me...	Може ли да ми помогнете…	*Mozhe li da mi pomognete...*
- cross the street?	- да пресека улицата?	*- da preseka ulitsata?*
- go up/down the stairs?	- да се кача/сляза по стълбите?	*- da se kacha/slyaza po stalbite?*
Can I sit down somewhere?	Може ли да седна някъде?	*Mozhe li da sedna nyakade?*

Could you call an accessible taxi for me?	Може ли да ми поръчате такси за инвалид?	*Mozhe li da mi porachate taksi za invalid?*

Repairs & cleaning

This is broken	Това е счупено	*Tova e schupeno*
Can you fix it?	Можете ли да го поправите?	*Mozhete li da go popravite?*
Do you have...	Имате ли...	*Imate li...*
- a battery?	- батерия?	*- bateriya?*
- spare parts?	- резервни части?	*- rezervni chasti?*
Can you... this?	Може ли... това?	*Mozhe li... tova?*
- clean	- да изчистите	*- da izchistite*
- press	- да изгладите	*- da izgladite*
- dry clean	- да изчистите химически	*- da izchistite himicheski*
- patch	- да закърпите	*- da zakarpite*
When will it be ready?	Кога ще е готово?	*Koga shte e gotovo?*
This isn't mine	Това не е мое	*Tova ne e moe*

Street dogs
These are still a very serious problem. Though most are friendly, attempts to pet them can result in a trip to hospital.

Tourist information

Where's the Tourist Information Office?	Къде е туристическият информационен център?	*Kade e turisticheskiyat informatsionen tsentar?*
Do you have a city/regional map?	Имате ли карта на града/региона?	*Imate li karta na grada/regiona?*

What are the main places of interest?	Кои са главните забележителности?	*Koi sa glavnite zabelezhitelnosti?*
Could you show me on the map?	Може ли да ми покажете на картата?	*Mozhe li da mi pokazhete na kartata?*
We'll be here for...	Ние сме тук за...	*Nie sme tuk za...*
- half a day	- половин ден	- *polovin den*
- a day	- един ден	- *edin den*
- a week	- една седмица	- *edna sedmitsa*
Do you have a brochure in English?	Имате ли брошура на английски?	*Imate li broshura na angliyski?*
We're interested in...	Ние се интересуваме от...	*Nie se interesuvame ot...*
- history	- история	- *istoriya*
- architecture	- архитектура	- *arhitektura*
- shopping	- пазаруване	- *pazaruvane*
- hiking	- планински туризъм	- *planinski turizam*
- a scenic walk	- панорамна разходка	- *panoramna razhodka*
- a boat cruise	- круиз с лодка	- *kruiz s lodka*
- a guided tour	- обиколка с екскурзовод	- *obikolka s ekskurzovod*
Are there any excursions?	Има ли някакви екскурзии?	*Ima li nyakakvi ekskurzii?*
How long does it take?	Колко време продължава?	*Kolko vreme prodalzhava?*
What does it cost?	Колко струва?	*Kolko struva?*
What days is it open/closed?	Кои дни е отворено/затворено?	*Koi dni e otvoreno/zatvoreno?*
What time does it open/close?	Кога отваря/затваря?	*Koga otvarya/zatvarya?*
What's the admission price?	Каква е входната такса?	*Kakva e vhodnata taksa?*
Are there any tours in English?	Има ли някакви обиколки на английски?	*Ima li nyakakvi obikolki na angliyski?*

Emergencies

Arranging health insurance before you visit Bulgaria is a very good idea. Emergency healthcare is free, but treatment and after-care might not be of the standard that visitors are accustomed to. Bulgarian doctors are highly qualified and competent but in some cases equipment and facilities are outdated. Private care may be desirable.

The loss or theft of a passport or valuables, a car accident, or any crime, should be reported immediately to the local police; it's also advisable to contact the embassy for information on local laws and procedures. The local authorities are entirely responsible for the investigation and prosecution of crimes.

Medical

Where is...	Къде е...	*Kade e...*
- the hospital?	- болницата?	*- bolnitsata?*
- the health centre?	- здравният център?	*- zdravniyat tsentar?*

I need...	Нуждая се от...	*Nuzhdaya se ot...*
- a doctor	- лекар	*- lekar*
- a female doctor	- лекарка	*- lekarka*
- an ambulance	- линейка	*- lineyka*

It's very urgent	Много е спешно	*Mnogo e speshno*
I'm injured	Имам нараняване	*Imam naranyavane*
Can I see a doctor?	Може ли да видя лекар?	*Mozhe li da vidya lekar?*
I don't feel well	Не се чувствам добре	*Ne se chuvstvam dobre*

I have...	Имам...	*Imam...*
- a cold	- простуда	*- prostuda*
- diarrhoea	- диария	*- diariya*
- a rash	- обрив	*- obriv*
- a temperature	- температура	*- temperatura*

I have a lump here	Имам бучка тук	*Imam buchka tuk*
It hurts here	Боли тук	*Boli tuk*
It hurts a lot/a little	Боли много/малко	*Boli mnogo/malko*

How much do I owe you?	Колко Ви дължа?	*Kolko vi dalzha?*
I have insurance	Имам застраховка	*Imam zastrahovka*

Dentist

I need a dentist	Нуждая се от зъболекар	*Nuzhdaya se ot zabolekar*
I have toothache	Боли ме зъб	*Boli me zab*
My gums are swollen	Венците ми са подути	*Ventsite mi sa poduti*
This filling has fallen out	Тази пломба е паднала	*Tazi plomba e padnala*
I have an abscess	Имам абцес	*Imam abtses*
I have broken a tooth	Счупих си зъб	*Schupih si zab*
Are you going to take it out?	Ще го извадите ли?	*Shte go izvadite li?*

| Can you fix it temporarily? | Може ли да го оправите временно? | *Mozhe li da go opravite vremenno?* |

Crime

I want to report a theft	Искам да съобщя за кражба	*Iskam da saobshtya za krazhba*
Someone has stolen my...	Някой открадна...	*Nyakoy otkradna...*
- bag	- чантата ми	*- chantata mi*
- car	- колата ми	*- kolata mi*
- credit cards	- кредитните ми карти	*- kreditnite mi karti*
- money	- парите ми	*- parite mi*
- passport	- паспорта ми	*- pasporta mi*

| I've been attacked | Бях нападнат | *Byah napadnat* |
| I've lost my... | Загубих си... | *Zagubih si...* |

Lost property

- car keys	- ключовете на колата	*- klyuchovete na kolata*
- driving licence	- шофьорската книжка	*- shofyorskata knizhka*
- handbag	- дамската чанта	*- damskata chanta*
- flight tickets	- самолетните билети	*- samoletnite bileti*

It happened...	Случи се...	*Sluchi se...*
- this morning	- тази сутрин	*- tazi sutrin*
- today	- днес	*- dnes*
- in the hotel	- в хотела	*- v hotela*

| I left it in the taxi | Забравих ги в таксито | *Zabravih gi v taksito* |

Breakdown

I've had...	Имах...	*Imah...*
- an accident	- произшествие	- *proizshestvie*
- a breakdown	- повреда	- *povreda*
- a puncture	- спукана гума	- *spukana guma*
My battery is flat	Акумулаторът ми е изтощен	*Akumulatorat mi e iztoshten*
I don't have a spare tyre	Нямам резервна гума	*Nyamam rezervna guma*
I've run out of petrol	Свършил съм бензина	*Svarshil sam benzina*
My car won't start	Колата ми не иска да запали	*Kolata mi ne iska da zapali*
Can you repair it?	Можете ли да я поправите?	*Mozhete li da ya popravite?*
How long will it take?	Колко време ще отнеме?	*Kolko vreme shte otneme?*
I have breakdown cover	Имам застраховка за повреда	*Imam zastrahovka za povreda*

Problems with the authorities

I'm sorry, I didn't realise...	Съжалявам, не разбрах, че...	*Sazhalyavam, ne razbrah, che...*
- I was driving so fast	- карам толкова бързо	- *karam tolkova barzo*
- I went over the red lights	- минах на червено	- *minah na cherveno*
- it was against the law	- нарушавам закона	- *narushavam zakona*
Here are my documents	Заповядайте, документите ми	*Zapovyadayte, dokumentite mi*
I'm innocent	Невинен съм	*Nevinen sam*

Emergency line 112
The emergency line 112 covers the whole country and is accessible from both standard and mobile phones. English-speaking operators are available.

Dictionary

This section consists of two parts:
an English-Bulgarian dictionary to
help you get your point across and
a Bulgarian-English one to decipher
the reply.

In Bulgarian there is no verbal
infinitive (eg "to walk"), so verbs
are given in the first person singular
(eg "I walk"). Nouns are not listed with
their gender, as there is no equivalent
of set articles (like "le" and "la" in
French). Plural forms vary depending
on the ending of the nouns and their
gender, but even then are irregular and
unpredictable – like most interesting
things in life!

English-Bulgarian dictionary

A

A&E	спешно отделение	*speshno otdelenie*
about (concerning)	за	*za*
accident	злополука	*zlopoluka*
accommodation	настаняване	*nastanyavane*
aeroplane	самолет	*samolet*
again	отново	*otnovo*
ago	преди	*predi*
AIDS	СПИН	*spin*
airmail	въздушна поща	*vazdushna poshta*
airport	летище	*letishte*
alarm	тревога	*trevoga*
all	всички	*vsichki*
all right	добре	*dobre*
allergy	алергия	*alergiya*
I am	съм	*sam*
ambulance	линейка	*lineyka*
America	Америка	*Amerika*
American	американски	*amerikanski*
and	и	*i*
anniversary	годишнина	*godishnina*
another	друг	*drug*
I answer	отговарям	*otgovaryam*
any	някой	*nyakoy*
apartment	апартамент	*apartament*
appointment	уговорка	*ugovorka*
April	април	*april*
area	област	*oblast*
area code	пощенски код	*poshtenski kod*
around	около, наоколо	*okolo, naokolo*
to arrange	уреждам	*urezhdam*
arrival	пристигане	*pristigane*

art	**изкуство**	***izkustvo***

Art lovers should browse Bulgarian shops – they still contain many affordable treasures.

I ask	питам	*pitam*
aspirin	аспирин	*aspirin*
at (time)	в	*v*
August	август	*avgust*
Australia	Австралия	*Avstraliya*
Australian	австралийски	*avstraliyski*
available	наличен	*nalichen*
away	далече	*daleche*

B

English	Bulgarian	Pronunciation
baby	бебе	bebe
back (body)	гръб	grab
back (place)	назад	nazad
bad	лош	losh
baggage	багаж	bagazh
bar (pub)	бар	bar
bath	баня	banya
beach	крайбрежие	kraybrezhie
because	защото	zashtoto
because of	поради	poradi
best	най-добър	nay-dobar
better	по-добър	po-dobar
between	между	mezhdu
bicycle	велосипед	velosiped
big	голям	golyam
bill	сметка	smetka
bit (a)	малко	malko
boarding card	бордна карта	bordna karta
book	книга	kniga
I book	резервирам	rezerviram
booking	резервация	rezervatsiya
box office	билетна каса	biletna kasa
boy	момче	momche
brother	брат	brat
bureau de change	обменно бюро	obmenno byuro
burned	изгорял	izgoryal
bus	автобус	avtobus
business	бизнес	biznes
but	но	no
I buy	купувам	kupuvam
by (air, car, etc)	с/със	s/sas
by (beside)	при	pri
by (via)	по	po

C

English	Bulgarian	Pronunciation
café	кафене	kafene
I call	обаждам се	obazhdam se
camera	фотоапарат	fotoaparat
I can	мога	moga
I cancel	отменям	otmenyam
car	автомобил	avtomobil
carnival	карнавал	karnaval
cash	пари в брой	pari v broy
cash point	банкомат	bankomat
casino	казино	kazino
castle	замък	zamak

cathedral	катедрала	*katedrala*

Sofia's multicultural centre has several Orthodox churches, a mosque and a synagogue, all within sight of each other.

CD	си ди	*si di*
centre	център	*tsentar*
I change	сменям	*smenyam*
charge	такса	*taksa*
I charge	таксувам	*taksuvam*
cheap	евтин	*evtin*
I check in (hotel, airport)	регистрирам се (в хотел, на летище)	*registriram se (v hotel, na letishte)*
cheque	чек	*chek*
child	дете	*dete*
I choose	избирам	*izbiram*
cigar	пура	*pura*
cigarette	цигара	*tsigara*
cinema	кино	*kino*
city	град	*grad*
I close	затварям	*zatvaryam*
close by	близо до	*blizo do*
closed	затворен	*zatvoren*
clothes	дрехи	*drehi*
club	клуб	*klub*
coast	бряг	*bryag*
coffee house	кафене	*kafene*
cold	студен	*student*
colour	цвят	*tsvyat*
I complain	оплаквам се	*oplakvam se*
complaint	оплакване	*oplakvane*
I confirm	потвърждавам	*potvarzhdavam*
confirmation	потвърждение	*potvarzhdenie*
consulate	консулство	*konsulstvo*
I contact	свързвам се с/със	*svarzvam se s/sus*
contagious	заразен	*zarazen*

cool	хладен	*hladen*

The Bulgarian slang word for "cool" is *gotin/a/o* (depending on the gender) and can describe anything from people to (hot) weather!

cost	цена	*tsena*
it costs	струва	*struva*
cot	бебешко легло	*bebeshko leglo*
country	страна	*strana*
countryside	провинция	*provintsiya*

| cream | крем | krem |
| credit card | кредитна карта | kreditna karta |

| **crime** | **престъпление** | *prestaplenie* |

In crowded areas, watch out for pickpockets trying your unzip your bag.

currency	валута	valuta
customer	клиент	klient
customs	митница	mitnitsa
cut	порязване	poryazvane
I cut	режа	rezha
cycling	карам велосипед	karam velosiped

D

damage	повреда	povreda
danger	опасност	opasnost
daughter	дъщеря	dashterya
day	ден	den
December	декември	dekemvri
dehydrated	обезводнен	obezvodnen
delay	забавяне	zabavyane
I dial	телефонирам	telefoniram
difficult	труден	truden
directions	указания/посоки	ukazaniya/posoki
dirty	мръсен	mrasen

| **disabled** | **инвалид** | *invalid* |

Only the newest buildings have facilities for those with disabilities. Pot-holed pavements can be a particular nightmare.

discount	отстъпка	otstapka
district	област	oblast
I disturb	безпокоя	bezpokoya
doctor	лекар	lekar
double	двоен	dvoen
down	долу	dolu
I drive	шофирам	shofiram
driver	шофьор	shofyor
driving licence	шофьорска книжка	shofyorska knizhka
drug	лекарство	lekarstvo
dry cleaner's	химическо чистене	himichesko chistene
during	по време на	po vreme na
duty (tax)	мито	mito

E

early	рано	*rano*
e-mail	имейл	*imeyl*
embassy	посолство	*posolstva*
emergency	спешен случай	*speshen sluchay*
England	Англия	*Angliya*
English	английски	*angliyski*
enough	достатъчно	*dostatachno*
entrance	вход	*vhod*
error	грешка	*greshka*
exactly	точно	*tochno*
exchange rate	обменен курс	*obmenen kurs*
exhibition	изложба	*izlozhba*
exit	изход	*izhod*
express (delivery)	експресен	*ekspresen*
express (train)	експресен	*ekspresen*

F

facilities	удобства	*udobstva*
far	далече	*daleche*
father	баща	*bashta*

| **favourite** | **любим** | ***lyubim*** |

One of Winston Churchill's favourite wines was Melnik. He ordered two barrels of it every year during World War II – even though Bulgaria was allied with Germany!

February	февруари	*fevruari*
festivals	фестивали	*festivali*
film (camera)	филм	*film*
film (cinema)	филм	*film*
fire	пожар	*pozhar*
fire exit	авариен изход	*avarien izhod*
first aid	първа помощ	*parva pomosht*
fitting room	пробна	*probna*
flight	полет	*polet*
flu	грип	*grip*
food poisoning	хранително отравяне	*hranitelno otravyane*
football	футбол	*futbol*
for	за	*za*
form (document)	формуляр	*formulyar*
free	свободен	*svoboden*
free (money)	безплатен	*bezplaten*
friend	приятел	*priyatel*
from	от	*ot*

G

gallery	галерия	galeriya
garage	гараж	garazh
gas	бензин	benzin
gents	мъже	mazhe
girl	момиче	momiche
glasses	очила	ochila
golf	голф	golf
golf course	голф игрище	golf igrishte
good	добър	dobar
group	група	grupa
guarantee	гаранция	garantsiya
guide	пътеводител	patevoditel

H

hair	коса	kosa
hairdresser's	фризьорски салон	frizyorski salon
half	половин	polovin
heat	жега	zhega
help!	помощ!	pomosht!
here	тук	tuk
high	висок	visok
holiday (work-free day)	почивен ден	pochiven den
holidays	ваканция	vakantsiya

| homosexual | хомосексуален | homoseksualen |

Although recent pro-gay legislation has been enacted, Bulgaria is not yet the best place to express same-sex affection in public.

hospital	болница	bolnitsa
hot	горещ	goresht
how?	как?	kak?
how big?	колко голям?	kolko golyam?
how far?	колко далече?	kolko daleche?
how long?	колко дълго?	kolko dalgo?
how much?	колко?	kolko?
hurry up!	побързай!	pobarzay!
husband	съпруг	saprug

I

identity card	лична карта	lichna karta
ill	болен	bolen
immediately	незабавно	nezabavno
important	важен	vazhen
in	в/във	v/vav

information	информация	*informatsiya*

Information from tourist centres tends to be outdated;
ordinary people are your best source of local advice.

inside	вътре	*vatre*
insurance	застраховка	*zastrahovka*
interesting	интересен	*interesen*
international	международен	*mezhdunaroden*
Ireland	Ирландия	*Irlandiya*
Irish	ирландски	*irlandski*
island	остров	*ostrov*
itinerary	маршрут	*marshrut*

J

January	януари	*yanuari*
jet ski	джет	*dzhet*
journey	пътешествие	*pateshestvie*
July	юли	*yuli*
junction	кръстовище	*krastovishte*
June	юни	*yuni*
just (only)	само	*samo*

K

key	ключ	*klyuch*
key ring	ключодържател	*klyuchodarzhatel*
keyboard	клавиатура	*klaviatura*
kid	дете	*dete*
kind (person)	мил, любезен	*mil/lyubezen*
kind (sort)	вид	*vid*
kiosk	павилион	*pavilion*
kiss	целувка	*tseluvka*

L

label	етикет	*etiket*
ladies (toilets)	жени	*zheni*
lady	дама	*dama*
lake	езеро	*ezero*
language	език	*ezik*
last	последен	*posleden*
late (delayed)	закъснял	*zakasnyal*
late (time)	късен	*kasen*
launderette	пералня	*peralnya*
lawyer	адвокат	*advokat*
less	по-малко	*po-malko*
library	библиотека	*biblioteka*
life jacket	спасителна жилетка	*spasitelna zhiletka*

lifeguard	бодигард	bodigard
lift	асансьор	asansyor
like	като	kato
little	малък	malak
local	местен	mesten
I lose	губя	gubya
lost property	изгубени вещи	izgubeni veshti
luggage	багаж	bagazh

M

madam	госпожа	gospozha
mail	поща	poshta
main	главен	glaven
man	мъж	mazh
manager	мениджър	menidzhar
many	много	mnogo
map (city)	карта	karta
map (road)	карта	karta

| March | март | mart |

March 1 is a big day and is celebrated by the giving of a tassel of red and white thread called a *martenitsa*. These symbolise health and good fortune.

market	пазар	pazar
married	семеен	semeen
May	май	may
maybe	може би	mozhe bi
mechanic	механичен	mehanichen
meeting	среща	sreshta
message	съобщение	saobshtenie
midday	пладне	pladne
midnight	полунощ	polunosht
minimum	минимум	minimum
minute	минута	minuta
missing	липсващ	lipsvasht
mobile phone	мобилен телефон	mobilen telefon
moment	момент	moment
money	пари	pari
more	повече	poveche
mosquito	комар	komar
most	най-много	nay-mnogo
mother	майка	mayka
much	много	mnogo
museum	музей	muzey
musical	музикален	muzikalen
must	трябва	tryabva
my	мой	moy

Dictionary N-O

English-Bulgarian

name	име	*ime*

Thanks to differences in the calendars of the old and new churches, people with saints' names often celebrate their name days twice.

nationality	националност	*natsionalnost*
near	близо	*blizo*
necessary	необходим	*neobhodim*
never	никога	*nikoga*
new	нов	*nov*
news	новина	*novina*
newspaper	вестник	*vestnik*
next	следващ	*sledvasht*
next to	до	*do*
nice	хубав	*hubav*
nice (people)	приятен	*priyaten*
night	нощ	*nosht*
nightclub	нощен клуб	*noshten klub*
north	север	*sever*
note (money)	банкнота	*banknota*
nothing	нищо	*nishto*
November	ноември	*noemvri*
now	сега	*sega*
nowhere	никъде	*nikade*
nudist beach	нудистки плаж	*nudistki plazh*
number (figure)	число	*chislo*
number (of items)	брой	*broy*

O

object	предмет	*predmet*
October	октомври	*oktomvri*
off (switched)	изключен	*izklyuchen*
office	офис	*ofis*
ok	окей	*okey*
on	на	*na*
once	веднъж	*vednazh*
only	само	*samo*
open	отворен	*otvoren*
I open	отварям	*otvaryam*
operator	оператор	*operator*
opposite (place)	насреща	*nasreshta*
optician's	оптика	*optika*
or	или	*ili*
other	друг	*drug*
out of order	развален	*razvalen*
outdoor	на открито	*na otkrito*

outside	навън	navan
overnight	за през нощта	za prez noshta
owner	собственик	sobstvenik
oxygen	кислород	kislorod

P

painkiller	обезболяващо	obezbolyavashto
pair	чифт	chift
parents	родители	roditeli
park	парк	park
parking	паркинг	parking
party	увеселение	uveselenie
passport	паспорт	pasport
people	хора	hora
perhaps	може би	mozhe bi
person	човек	chovek
petrol	бензин/петрол	benzin/petrol
petrol station	бензиностанция	benzinostantsiya

| **photo** | **снимка** | **snimka** |

Taking a photo in a Bulgarian museum is a furtive adventure, as each has a snapping ban for security reasons.

phrase book	разговорник	razgovornik
place	място	myasto
platform	перон	peron
police	полиция	politsiya
port (sea)	пристанище	pristanishte
possible	възможен	vazmozhen
post	поща	poshta
post office	пощенски офис	poshtenski ofis
prescription	рецепта	retsepta
price	цена	tsena
private	частен	chasten
probably	вероятно	veroyatno
problem	проблем	problem
pub	кръчма	krachma
public transport	обществен транспорт	obshtestven transport

Q

quality	качество	kachestvo
quantity	количество	kolichestvo
query	запитване; въпросителен знак	zapitvane; vaprositelen znak
question	въпрос	vapros
queue	опашка	opashka

quick	бърз	*barz*
quickly	бързо	*barzo*
quiet	тих	*tih*
quite	съвсем	*savsem*
quiz	шега	*shega*

R

radio	радио	*radio*
railway	железница	*zheleznitsa*
rain	дъжд	*dazhd*
rape	насилие	*nasilie*
ready	готов	*gotov*
real	истински	*istinski*
receipt	квитанция	*kvitantsiya*
receipt (shopping)	касова бележка	*kasova belezhka*
reception	рецепция	*retseptsiya*
receptionist	рецепционист	*retseptsionist*
reduction	намаление	*namalenie*

---

refund	**възстановяване на сума**	*vazstanovyavane na suma*

Do be aware that it can be tricky to return or exchange
goods, even on production of a receipt.

I relax	почивам	*pochivam*
rent	наем	*naem*
I rent	наемам	*naemam*
reservation	резервация	*rezervatsiya*
retired	пенсиониран	*pensioniran*
rich	богат	*bogat*

---

road	**път**	*pat*

Crossing the road can be a challenge: few drivers
heed traffic lights and zebra crossings are regarded
as mere highway decoration.

---

room	стая	*staya*
route	маршрут	*marshrut*
rude	груб	*grub*
ruins	развалини	*razvalini*
I run	тичам	*ticham*

S

sauna	сауна	*sauna*
Scotland	Шотландия	*Shotlandiya*
Scottish	шотландски	*shotlandski*
sea	море	*more*

seat	място	*myasto*
seat belt	**предпазен колан**	*predpazen kolan*
sedative	**успокоително**	*uspokoitelno*
see you later!	**довиждане**	*dovizhdane*
self-service	**самообслужване**	*samoobsluzhvane*
September	**септември**	*septemvri*
service	**обслужване**	*obsluzhvane*
shop	**магазин**	*magazin*
shopping	**пазаруване**	*pazaruvane*
shopping centre	**търговски център**	*targovski tsentar*
short	**къс**	*kas*
I show	**показвам**	*pokazvam*
shut	**затворен**	*zatvoren*
sign	**знак**	*znak*
signature	**подпис**	*podpis*
since	**оттогава**	*ottogava*
sir	**господин**	*gospodin*
sister	**сестра**	*sestra*
ski	**ски**	*ski*
sleeping pill	**приспивателно**	*prispivatelno*
slow	**бавен**	*baven*
small	**малък**	*malak*
soft	**мек**	*mek*
some	**няколко**	*nyakolko*
something	**нещо**	*neshto*
son	**син**	*sin*
soon	**скоро**	*skoro*
south	**юг**	*yug*
South Africa	**Южна Африка**	*Yuzhna Afrika*
South African	**южноафриканец**	*yuzhnoafrikanets*

speed	**скорост**	***skorost***

Police checks for observing the speed limits, using seat belts and alcohol tests on major roads are common and transgressors get an on-the-spot fine.

sport	**спорт**	*sport*
stadium	**стадион**	*stadion*
staff	**персонал**	*personal*
stamp	**печат**	*pechat*
station	**гара, станция**	*gara, stantsiya*
sterling (pound)	**английска лира**	*angliyska lira*
straight	**направо**	*napravo*
street	**улица**	*ulitsa*
stress	**ударение**	*udarenie*
suitcase	**куфар**	*kufar*
sun	**слънце**	*slantse*
sunglasses	**слънчеви очила**	*slanchevi ochila*

surname	презиме	*prezime*
swimming pool	плувен басейн	*pluven baseyn*
switched on	включен	*vklyuchen*
symptom	симптом	*simptom*

T

table	маса	*masa*
I take	вземам	*vzemam*
tampons	тампони	*tampon*

| **tax** | **данък** | *danak* |

In Ottoman days, sons were given to the army as a form of tax payment.

tax free	освободен от данък	*osvoboden ot danak*
taxi	такси	*taksi*
telephone	телефон	*telefon*
telephone box	телефонна кабина	*telefonna kabina*
television	телевизия	*televiziya*
tennis	тенис	*tenis*
tennis court	тенис корт	*tenis kort*
text	текст	*tekst*
that	онова	*onova*
theft	кражба	*krazhba*
then	тогава	*togava*
there	там	*tam*
thing	нещо	*neshto*
I think	мисля	*mislya*
thirsty	жаден	*zhaden*
this	това	*tova*
through	през	*prez*
ticket (bus)	билет	*bilet*
ticket (cinema)	билет	*bilet*
ticket (parking)	квитанция	*kvitantsiya*
ticket office	билетно гише	*biletno gishe*
time (clock)	време	*vreme*
timetable	разписание	*razpisanie*

| **tip (money)** | **бакшиш** | *bakshish* |

Taxi drivers and waiters expect a 10 to 15 per cent tip; donors should not expect gratitude.

tired	уморен	*umoren*
to	към	*kam*
to (the left/right)	на (ляво/дясно)	*na (lyavo/dyasno)*
today	днес	*dnes*
toilet	тоалетна	*toaletna*

toiletries	тоалетни принадлежности	*toaletni prinadlezhnosti*
toll	такса	*taksa*
tomorrow	утре	*utre*
tonight	довечера	*dovechera*
too	също	*sashto*
tourist office	туристически офис	*turisticheski ofis*
town	град	*grad*
town hall	кметство	*kmetstvo*
train	влак	*vlak*
tram	трамвай	*tramvay*
I translate	превеждам	*prevezhdam*
I travel	пътувам	*patuvam*
travel agency	пътническа агенция	*patnicheska agentsiya*
true (right)	верен	*veren*
typical	типичен	*tipichen*

U

ulcer	язва	*yazva*
umbrella	чадър	*chadar*
uncomfortable	неудобен	*neudoben*
unconscious	в безсъзнание	*v bezsaznanie*
under	под	*pod*
underground (metro)	метро	*metro*
I understand	разбирам	*razbiram*
underwear	бельо	*belyo*
unemployed	безработен	*bezraboten*
unpleasant	неприятен	*nepriyaten*
up	нагоре	*nagore*
upstairs	горе	*gore*
urgent	спешен	*speshen*
I use	използвам	*izpolzvam*
useful	полезен	*polezen*
usually	обикновено	*obiknoveno*

V

vacant	свободен	*svoboden*
vacation	ваканция	*vakantsiya*
vaccination	ваксинация	*vaksinatsiya*
valid	валиден	*validen*
valuables	ценности	*tsennosti*
value	стойност	*stoynost*
VAT	ДДС	*de de se*

vegetarian	вегетарианец	*vegetarianets*

Christmas Eve dinner consists only of vegetarian dishes.
Leftovers stay on the table overnight... for the dead.

vehicle	превозно средство	*prevozno sredstvo*
very	много	*mnogo*
visa	виза	*viza*
visit	посещение	*poseshtenie*
I visit	посещавам	*poseshtavam*
vitamin	витамин	*vitamin*
I vomit	повръщам	*povrashtam*

W

waiter/waitress	сервитьор/ка	*servityor/ka*
waiting room	чакалня	*chakalnya*
Wales	Уелс	*uels*
I walk	ходя	*hodya*
wallet	портмоне	*portmone*
I want	искам	*iskam*
I wash	мия	*miya*
watch	часовник	*chasovnik*
water	вода	*voda*
water sports	водни спортове	*vodni sportove*
way (manner)	начин	*nachin*
way (route)	път	*pat*
way in	вход	*vhod*
way out	изход	*izhod*
weather	време	*vreme*
web	страница	*stranitsa*
website	уебсайт	*uebsayt*
week	седмица	*sedmitsa*
weekday	делничен ден	*delnichen den*
weekend	уикенд	*uikend*
welcome	добре дошъл	*dobre doshal*
well	добре	*dobre*
west	запад	*zapad*
what	какво	*kakvo*
wheelchair	инвалидна количка	*invalidna kolichka*

when	**кога**	*koga*

Any question starting with "when?" will elicit a response of *ey sega*. This can mean anything from "immediately" to "in the next thousand years".

where	къде	*kade*
which	кой/коя/кое	*koy/koya/koe*
while	докато	*dokato*
who	кой	*koy*
why	защо	*zashto*
wife	съпруга	*sapruga*

wine	вино	_vino_
with	с/със	s/sas
without	без	bez

woman	**жена**	**zhena**

Bulgarian women pull off the career/family balance with panache, and even dress up before putting the washing out.

wonderful	чудесен	chudesen
word	дума	duma
work	работа	rabota
I work	работя	rabotya
it works	работи	raboti
world	свят	svyat
worried	притеснен	pritesnen
I write	пиша	pisha
wrong (mistaken)	грешен	greshen

X

| x-ray | рентгенов | rentgenov |

Y

yacht	яхта	yahta
year	година	godina
yearly	годишен	godishen
yellow pages	жълти страници	zhalti stranitsi
yes	да	da
yesterday	вчера	vchera
yet	още	oshte
you (formal)	Вие	vie
you (informal)	ти	ti
young	млад	mlad
your (formal)	Ваш	vash
your (informal)	твой	tvoy
youth hostel	хостел	hostel

Z

zebra crossing	пешеходна пътека	peshehodna pateka
zero	нула	nula
zone	зона	zona
zoo	зоологическа градина	zoologicheska gradina

Bulgarian-English dictionary

А

аварien изход	*avarien izhod*	fire exit
август	*avgust*	August
австралийски	*avstraliyski*	Australian
Австралия	*Avstraliya*	Australia
автобус	*avtobus*	bus
автомобил	*avtomobil*	car
адвокат	*advokat*	lawyer
алергия	*alergiya*	allergy
Америка	*Amerika*	America

американски	***amerikanski***	**American**

Sirni Zagovezni is similar to the American Thanksgiving Day.

английска лира	*angliyska lira*	sterling (pound)
английски	*angliyski*	English
Англия	*Angliya*	England
апартамент	*apartament*	apartment
април	*april*	April
асансьор	*asansyor*	lift
аспирин	*aspirin*	aspirin

Б

бавен	*baven*	slow
багаж	*bagazh*	baggage
багаж	*bagazh*	luggage
бакшиш	*bakshish*	tip (money)
банкнота	*banknota*	note (money)
банкомат	*bankomat*	cash point
баня	*banya*	bath
бар	*bar*	bar (pub)
баща	*bashta*	father
бебе	*bebe*	baby
бебешко легло	*bebeshko leglo*	cot
без	*bez*	without
безплатен	*bezplaten*	free (money)
безпокоя	*bezpokoya*	I disturb
безработен	*bezraboten*	unemployed
бельо	*belyo*	underwear
бензин	*benzin*	gas
бензиностанция	*benzinostantsiya*	petrol station
библиотека	*biblioteka*	library
бизнес	*biznes*	business
билет	*bilet*	ticket (bus)
билет	*bilet*	ticket (cinema)
билетна каса	*biletna kasa*	box office

билетно гише	biletno gishe	ticket office
близо	blizo	near
близо до	blizo do	close by
богат	bogat	rich
бодигард	bodigard	lifeguard
болен	bolen	ill
болница	bolnitsa	hospital
брат	brat	brother
брой	broy	number (items)
бряг	bryag	coast
бърз	barz	quick
бързо	barzo	quickly

В

в	v	at (time)
в безсъзнание	v bezsaznanie	unconscious
в/във	v/vav	in
важен	vazhen	important
ваканция	vakantsiya	holidays
ваканция	vakantsiya	vacation
ваксинация	vaksinatsiya	vaccination
валиден	validen	valid
валута	valuta	currency
Ваш	vash	your (formal)
вегетарианец	vegetarianets	vegetarian
веднъж	vednazh	once
велосипед	velosiped	bicycle
вероятно	veroyatno	probably
вестник	vestnik	newspaper
вземам	vzemam	I take
вид	vid	kind (sort)
Вие	vie	you (formal)
виза	viza	visa
вино	vino	wine
висок	visok	high
витамин	vitamin	vitamin
включен	vklyuchen	switched on
влак	vlak	train

| **вода** | **voda** | **water** |

A Bulgarian good luck tradition is to throw water along with a bunch of geraniums.

водни спортове	vodni sportove	water sports
време	vreme	time (clock)
време	vreme	weather
всички	vsichki	all
вход	vhod	entrance/way in
вчера	vchera	yesterday
въздушна поща	vazdushna poshta	airmail

възможен	*vazmozhen*	possible
възстановяване на сума	*vazstanovyavane na suma*	refund
въпрос	*vapros*	question
вътре	*vatre*	inside

Г

галерия	*galeriya*	gallery
гара, станция	*gara, stantsiya*	station
гараж	*garazh*	garage
гаранция	*garantsiya*	guarantee
главен	*glaven*	main
година	*godina*	year
годишен	*godishen*	yearly
годишнина	*godishnina*	anniversary
голф	*golf*	golf
голф игрище	*golf igrishte*	golf course
голям	*golyam*	big
горе	*gore*	upstairs
горещ	*goresht*	hot
господин	*gospodin*	sir
госпожа	*gospozha*	madam
готов	*gotov*	ready
град	*grad*	city/town
грешен	*greshen*	wrong (mistaken)
грешка	*greshka*	error
грип	*grip*	flu
група	*grupa*	group

| груб | ***grub*** | rude |

Locals use the particles "*ma*" and "*be*" at the end of certain statements. This is considered to be rude.

| гръб | *grab* | back (body) |
| губя | *gubya* | I lose |

Д

да	*da*	yes
далече	*daleche*	away
далече	*daleche*	far
дама	*dama*	lady
данък	*danak*	tax
двоен	*dvoen*	double
ДДС	*de de se*	VAT
декември	*dekemvri*	December
делничен ден	*delnichen den*	weekday
ден	*den*	day
дете	*dete*	child
джет	*dzhet*	jet ski

днес	*dnes*	today
до	*do*	next to
добре	*do<u>bre</u>*	all right
добре	*do<u>bre</u>*	well
добре дошъл	*do<u>bre</u> do<u>sh</u>al*	welcome
добър	*do<u>bar</u>*	good
довечера	*dove<u>che</u>ra*	tonight

довиждане   ***do<u>vizh</u>dane***   **see you later!**
Actually, the Italian greeting "ciao" has become the most common way of saying goodbye.

докато	*doka<u>to</u>*	while
долу	*do<u>lu</u>*	down
достатъчно	*dos<u>ta</u>tachno*	enough
дрехи	*<u>dre</u>hi*	clothes
друг	*drug*	another
друг	*drug*	other
дума	*<u>du</u>ma*	word
дъжд	*dazhd*	rain
дъщеря	*dashter<u>ya</u>*	daughter

Е

евтин	*<u>ev</u>tin*	cheap

езеро   ***<u>e</u>zero***   **lake**
Bulgarian mountain regions are stunning, with clear blue lakes and rugged, snow-capped peaks.

език	*e<u>zik</u>*	language
експресен	*eks<u>pre</u>sen*	express (delivery)
експресен	*eks<u>pre</u>sen*	express (train)
етикет	*eti<u>ket</u>*	label
жаден	*<u>zha</u>den*	thirsty
жега	*<u>zhe</u>ga*	heat
железница	*zhe<u>lez</u>nitsa*	railway
жена	*zhe<u>na</u>*	woman
жени	*zhe<u>ni</u>*	ladies (toilets)
жълти страници	*<u>zhal</u>ti <u>stra</u>nitsi*	yellow pages

З

за	*za*	about (concerning)
за	*za*	for
за през нощта	*za prez nosh<u>ta</u>*	overnight
забавяне	*za<u>ba</u>vyane*	delay
закъснял	*zakas<u>nyal</u>*	late (delayed)
замък	*<u>za</u>mak*	castle
запад	*<u>za</u>pad*	west
заразен	*za<u>ra</u>zen*	contagious

застраховка	*zastrahovka*	insurance
затварям	*zatvaryam*	I close
затворен	*zatvoren*	closed
затворен	*zatvoren*	shut
защо	*zashto*	why
защото	*zashtoto*	because
злополука	*zlopoluka*	accident
знак	*znak*	sign
зона	*zona*	zone
зоологическа градина	*zoologicheska gradina*	zoo

И

и	*i*	and
избирам	*izbiram*	I choose
изгорял	*izgoryal*	burned
изгубени вещи	*izgubeni veshti*	lost property
изключен	*izklyuchen*	off (switched)
изкуство	*izkustvo*	art
изложба	*izlozhba*	exhibition
използвам	*izpolzvam*	I use
изход	*izhod*	exit
изход	*izhod*	way out
или	*ili*	or
име	*ime*	name
имейл	*imeyl*	e-mail
инвалид	*invalid*	disabled
инвалидна количка	*invalidna kolichka*	wheelchair
интересен	*interesen*	interesting
информация	*informatsiya*	information
Ирландия	*Irlandiya*	Ireland
ирландски	*irlandski*	Irish
искам	*iskam*	I want
истински	*istinski*	real

К

казино	*kazino*	casino
как	*kak*	how
какво	*kakvo*	what

| **карам велосипед** | ***karam velosiped*** | **cycling** |
| Cycling is the best way to travel around rural areas. | | |

карнавал	*karnaval*	carnival
карта	*karta*	map (city)
карта	*karta*	map (road)
касова бележка	*kasova belezhka*	receipt (shopping)
катедрала	*katedrala*	cathedral

като	*kato*	like
кафене	*kafene*	café/coffee house
качество	*kachestvo*	quality
квитанция	*kvitantsiya*	receipt
квитанция	*kvitantsiya*	ticket (parking)
кино	*kino*	cinema
кислород	*kislorod*	oxygen
клавиатура	*klaviatura*	keyboard
клиент	*klient*	customer
клуб	*klub*	club
ключ	*klyuch*	key
ключодържател	*klyuchodarzhatel*	key ring
кметство	*kmetstvo*	town hall
книга	*kniga*	book
кога	*koga*	when
кой	*koy*	who
кой/коя/кое	*koy/koya/koe*	which

| **количество** | ***kolichestvo*** | **quantity** |

In most restaurants, menus give a meal's weight. This is very useful as a guide to what quantity you will get.

колко голям?	*kolko golyam?*	how big?
колко далече?	*kolko daleche?*	how far?
колко дълго?	*kolko dalgo?*	how long?
колко?	*kolko?*	how much?
комар	*komar*	mosquito
консулство	*konsulstvo*	consulate
коса	*kosa*	hair
кражба	*krazhba*	theft
крайбрежие	*kraybrezhie*	beach
кредитна карта	*kreditna karta*	credit card
крем	*krem*	cream
кръстовище	*krastovishte*	junction
кръчма	*krachma*	pub
купувам	*kupuvam*	I buy
куфар	*kufar*	suitcase
къде	*kade*	where
към	*kam*	to

| **къс** | ***kas*** | **short** |

There are many short Bulgarian words, but the longest one is 'непротивоконституционствувателствувайте' ("do not act against the constitution").

| късен | *kasen* | late (time) |

лекар	lekar	doctor
лекарство	lekarstvo	drug
летище	letishte	airport
линейка	lineyka	ambulance
липсващ	lipsvasht	missing
лична карта	lichna karta	identity card
лош	losh	bad
любим	lyubim	favourite

М

магазин	magazin	shop
май	may	May
майка	mayka	mother
малко	malko	bit (a)

| **малък** | **malak** | **little/small** |

The little country of Bulgaria contains 376 political parties.

март	mart	March
маршрут	marshrut	itinerary
маршрут	marshrut	route
маса	masa	table
между	mezhdu	between
международен	mezhdunaroden	international
мек	mek	soft
мениджър	menidzhar	manager
местен	mesten	local
метро	metro	underground (metro)
механичен	mehanichen	mechanic
мил, любезен	mil/lyubezen	kind (person)
минимум	minimum	minimum
минута	minuta	minute
мисля	mislya	I think
митница	mitnitsa	customs
мито	mito	duty (tax)
мия	miya	I wash
млад	mlad	young
много	mnogo	many
много	mnogo	much
много	mnogo	very
мобилен телефон	mobilen telefon	mobile phone
мога	moga	I can
може би	mozhe bi	maybe
може би	mozhe bi	perhaps
мой	moy	my
момент	moment	moment
момиче	momiche	girl
момче	momche	boy

море	*more*	sea
мръсен	*mrasen*	dirty
музей	*muzey*	museum

| музикален | *muzikalen* | musical |

One of the many traditional musical instruments is the *gayda*, a goat-skin bagpipe.

мъж	*mazh*	man
мъже	*mazhe*	gents (toilets)
място	*myasto*	place
място	*myasto*	seat

Н

на	*na*	on
на (ляво/дясно)	*na (lyavo/dyasno)*	to (the left/right)
на открито	*na otkrito*	outdoor
навън	*navan*	outside
нагоре	*nagore*	up
наем	*naem*	rent
наемам	*naemam*	I rent
назад	*nazad*	back (place)
най-добър	*nay-dobar*	best
най-много	*nay-mnogo*	most
наличен	*nalichen*	available
намаление	*namalenie*	reduction
направо	*napravo*	straight
насилие	*nasilie*	rape
насреща	*nasreshta*	opposite (place)
настаняване	*nastanyavane*	accommodation
националност	*natsionalnost*	nationality
начин	*nachin*	way (manner)
незабавно	*nezabavno*	immediately
необходим	*neobhodim*	necessary
неприятен	*nepriyaten*	unpleasant
неудобен	*neudoben*	uncomfortable
нещо	*neshto*	something
нещо	*neshto*	thing
никога	*nikoga*	never
никъде	*nikade*	nowhere
нищо	*nishto*	nothing
но	*no*	but
нов	*nov*	new

| новина | *novina* | news |

The good news is that there are about 9,000 identical words in English and Bulgarian that sound the same and mean the same thing.

ноември	*noemvri*	November
нощ	*nosht*	night
нощен клуб	*noshten klub*	nightclub
нудистки плаж	*nudistki plazh*	nudist beach
нула	*nula*	zero
някой	*nyakoy*	any
няколко	*nyakolko*	some

О

обаждам се	*obazhdam se*	I call
обезболяващо	*obezbolyavashto*	painkiller
обезводнявам	*obezvodnyavam*	I dehydrate
обикновено	*obiknoveno*	usually
област	*oblast*	area
област	*oblast*	district
обменен курс	*obmenen kurs*	exchange rate
обменно бюро	*obmenno byuro*	bureau de change
обслужване	*obsluzhvane*	service
обществен транспорт	*obshtestven transport*	public transport
около, наоколо	*okolo, naokolo*	around
октомври	*oktomvri*	October
онова	*onova*	that
опасност	*opasnost*	danger
опашка	*opashka*	queue
оператор	*operator*	operator
оплаквам се	*oplakvam se*	I complain
оплакване	*oplakvane*	complaint
оптика	*optika*	optician's
освободен от данък	*osvoboden ot danak*	tax free
остров	*ostrov*	island
от	*ot*	from
отварям	*otvaryam*	I open
отворен	*otvoren*	open
отговарям	*otgovaryam*	I answer
отменям	*otmenyam*	I cancel
отново	*otnovo*	again
отстъпка	*otstapka*	discount
оттогава	*ottogava*	since
офис	*ofis*	office
очила	*ochila*	glasses
още	*oshte*	yet

П

павилион	*pavilion*	kiosk
пазар	*pazar*	market
пазаруване	*pazaruvane*	shopping
пари	*pari*	money

пари в брой	_pari v broy_	cash
парк	_park_	park
паркинг	_parking_	parking
паспорт	_pasport_	passport
пенсиониран	_pensioniran_	retired
пералня	_peralnya_	launderette
перон	_peron_	platform
персонал	_personal_	staff
петрол	_petrol_	petrol
печат	_pechat_	stamp
пешеходна пътека	_peshehodna pateka_	zebra crossing
питам	_pitam_	I ask
пиша	_pisha_	I write
пладне	_pladne_	midday
плувен басейн	_pluven baseyn_	swimming pool
по	_po_	by (via)

| по време на | _po vreme na_ | during |

During Bulgarian weddings, the couple step on each other's feet to see who will be boss indoors.

побързай!	_pobarzay!_	hurry up!
повече	_poveche_	more
повреда	_povreda_	damage
повръщам	_povrashtam_	I vomit
под	_pod_	under
подпис	_podpis_	signature
пожар	_pozhar_	fire
показвам	_pokazvam_	I show
полезен	_polezen_	useful
полет	_polet_	flight
полиция	_politsiya_	police
половин	_polovin_	half
полунощ	_polunosht_	midnight
по-малко	_po-malko_	less
помощ!	_pomosht!_	help!
поради	_poradi_	because of
портмоне	_portmone_	wallet
порязване	_poryazvane_	cut
посещавам	_poseshtavam_	I visit
посещение	_poseshtenie_	visit
последен	_posleden_	last
посолство	_posolstvo_	embassy
потвърждавам	_potvarzhdavam_	I confirm
потвърждение	_potvarzhdenie_	confirmation
почивам	_pochivam_	I relax
почивен ден	_pochiven den_	holiday (work-free day)
поща	_poshta_	mail/post

пощенски код	*poshtenski kod*	area code
пощенски офис	*poshtenski ofis*	post office
превозно средство	*prevozno sredstvo*	vehicle

| превеждам | *prevezhdam* | to translate |

Some strange translations you may see on menus include "fumigated" (smoked) cheese and "constipated" (roast) potatoes.

преди	*predi*	ago
предмет	*predmet*	object
предпазен колан	*predpazen kolan*	seat belt
през	*prez*	through
презиме	*prezime*	surname
престъпление	*prestaplenie*	crime
при	*pri*	by (beside)
приспивателно	*prispivatelno*	sleeping pill
пристанище	*pristanishte*	port (sea)
пристигане	*pristigane*	arrival
притеснен	*pritesnen*	worried
приятел	*priyatel*	friend
приятен	*priyaten*	nice (people)
проблем	*problem*	problem
пробна	*probna*	fitting room
провинция	*provintsiya*	countryside
пура	*pura*	cigar
първа помощ	*parva pomosht*	first aid
път	*pat*	road
път	*pat*	way (route)
пътеводител	*patevoditel*	guide
пътешествие	*pateshestvie*	journey
пътническа агенция	*patnicheska agentsiya*	travel agency
пътувам	*patuvam*	I travel

Р

работа	*rabota*	work
работи	*raboti*	it works
работя	*rabotya*	I work
радио	*radio*	radio
разбирам	*razbiram*	I understand
развален	*razvalen*	out of order
развалини	*razvalini*	ruins
разговорник	*razgovornik*	phrase book
разписание	*razpisanie*	timetable
рано	*rano*	early
регистрирам се (в хотел, на летище)	*registriram se (v hotel, na letishte)*	I check in (hotel, airport)

режа	*rezha*	to cut

Bulgarians usually use a knife only when the food needs to be cut; otherwise they eat solely with a fork.

резервация	*rezervatsiya*	booking
резервация	*rezervatsiya*	reservation
резервирам	*rezerviram*	I book
рентгенов	*rentgenov*	x-ray
рецепта	*retsepta*	prescription
рецепционист	*retseptsionist*	receptionist
рецепция	*retseptsiya*	reception
родители	*roditeli*	parents

С

с/със	*s/sas*	by/with
само	*samo*	just/only
самолет	*samolet*	aeroplane
самообслужване	*samoobsluzhvane*	self-service
сауна	*sauna*	sauna
свободен	*svoboden*	free/vacant
свят	*svyat*	world
север	*sever*	north
сега	*sega*	now
седмица	*sedmitsa*	week
семеен	*semeen*	married
септември	*septemvri*	September
сервитьор/ка	*servityor/ka*	waiter/waitress
сестра	*sestra*	sister
си ди	*si di*	CD
симптом	*simptom*	symptom
син	*sin*	son

ски	*ski*	ski

Bulgaria boasts magnificent runs and facilities for ski enthusiasts at prices that are much cheaper than Alpine resorts.

скоро	*skoro*	soon
скорост	*skorost*	speed
следващ	*sledvasht*	next
слънце	*slantse*	sun
слънчеви очила	*slanchevi ochila*	sunglasses
сменям	*smenyam*	I change
сметка	*smetka*	bill
снимка	*snimka*	photo
собственик	*sobstvenik*	owner

спасителна жилетка	*spasitelna zhiletka*	life jacket
спешен	*speshen*	urgent
спешен случай	*speshen sluchay*	emergency
СПИН	*spin*	AIDS
спорт	*sport*	sport
среща	*sreshta*	meeting
стадион	*stadion*	stadium
стая	*staya*	room
стойност	*stoynost*	value
страна	*strana*	country
страница	*stranitsa*	web
струва	*struva*	it costs
студен	*student*	cold
съвсем	*savsem*	quite
съм	*sam*	I am
съобщение	*saobshtenie*	message
съпруг	*saprug*	husband
съпруга	*sapruga*	wife
също	*sashto*	too

Т

такса	*taksa*	charge/toll
такси	*taksi*	taxi
таксувам	*taksuvam*	I charge
там	*tam*	there
тампони	*tampon*	tampons
твой	*tvoy*	your (informal)
текст	*tekst*	text
телевизия	*televiziya*	television
телефон	*telefon*	telephone
телефонирам	*telefoniram*	I dial
телефонна кабина	*telefonna kabina*	telephone box
тенис	*tenis*	tennis
тенис корт	*tenis kort*	tennis court
ти	*ti*	you (informal)

типичен	***tipichen***	**typical**

One typical southeastern Bulgarian ritual is a barefoot
dance on embers that's accompanied by the beat of the
sacred drum.

тих	*tih*	quiet
тичам	*ticham*	I run
тоалетна	*toaletna*	toilet
тоалетни принадлежности	*toaletni prinadlezhnosti*	toiletries
това	*tova*	this

тогава	*togava*	then
точно	*tochno*	exactly
трамвай	*tramvay*	tram
тревога	*trevoga*	alarm
труден	*truden*	difficult
трябва	*tryabva*	must
тук	*tuk*	here
туристически офис	*turisticheski ofis*	tourist office
търговски център	*targovski tsentar*	shopping centre

У

увеселение	*uveselenie*	party
уговорка	*ugovorka*	appointment
ударение	*udarenie*	stress
удобства	*udobstva*	facilities
уебсайт	*uebsayt*	website
Уелс	*uels*	Wales
уикенд	*uikend*	weekend
указания/посоки	*ukazaniya/posoki*	directions
улица	*ulitsa*	street
уморен	*umoren*	tired
уреждам	*urezhdam*	I arrange
успокоително	*uspokoitelno*	sedative
утре	*utre*	tomorrow

Ф

| февруари | *fevruari* | February |

фестивали **festivali** **festivals**
One of the most spectacular folk festivals, *kukeri*, sees men in hairy head-dresses performing dances to ward off evil.

филм	*film*	film (camera/cinema)
формуляр	*formulyar*	form (document)
фотоапарат	*fotoaparat*	camera
фризьорски салон	*frizyorski salon*	hairdresser's
футбол	*futbol*	football

Х

химическо чистене	*himichesko chistene*	dry cleaner's
хладен	*hladen*	cool
ходя	*hodya*	I walk
хомосексуален	*homoseksualen*	homosexual
хора	*hora*	people
хостел	*hostel*	youth hostel
хранително отравяне	*hranitelno otravyane*	food poisoning

93

хубав	*hubav*	nice

Ц

цвят	*tsvyat*	colour
целувка	*tseluvka*	kiss
цена	*tsena*	cost/price
ценности	*tsennosti*	valuables
център	*tsentar*	centre
цигара	*tsigara*	cigarette

Ч

чадър	*chadar*	umbrella
чакалня	*chakalnya*	waiting room
часовник	*chasovnik*	watch
частен	*chasten*	private
чек	*chek*	cheque
число	*chislo*	number (figure)
чифт	*chift*	pair
човек	*chovek*	person
чудесен	*chudesen*	wonderful

Ш

шега	*shega*	quiz
Шотландия	*Shotlandiya*	Scotland
шотландски	*shotlandski*	Scottish

шофирам	***shofiram***	**I drive**

If you're driving in Bulgaria, the speed limit in the towns and villages is 50 km/h; outside built-up areas it's 80 km/h, and on the highways 130 km/h.

шофьор	*shofyor*	driver
шофьорска книжка	*shofyorska knizhka*	driving licence

Ю

юг	*yug*	south
Южна Африка	*Yuzhna Afrika*	South Africa
южноафриканец	*yuzhnoafrikanets*	South African
юли	*yuli*	July
юни	*yuni*	June

Я

язва	*yazva*	ulcer
януари	*yanuari*	January
яхта	*yahta*	yacht

Quick reference

Numbers

0	**Нула**	_Nula_
1	**Едно**	_Edno_
2	**Две**	_Dve_
3	**Три**	_Tri_
4	**Четири**	_Chetiri_
5	**Пет**	_Pet_
6	**Шест**	_Shest_
7	**Седем**	_Sedem_
8	**Осем**	_Osem_
9	**Девет**	_Devet_
10	**Десет**	_Deset_
11	**Единадесет**	_Edinadeset_
12	**Дванадесет**	_Dvanadeset_
13	**Тринадесет**	_Trinadeset_
14	**Четиринадесет**	_Chetirinadeset_
15	**Петнадесет**	_Petnadeset_
16	**Шестнадесет**	_Shestnadeset_
17	**Седемнадесет**	_Sedemnadeset_
18	**Осемнадесет**	_Osemnadeset_
19	**Деветнадесет**	_Devetnadeset_
20	**Двадесет**	_Dvadeset_
21	**Двадесет и едно**	_Dvadeset i edno_
30	**Тридесет**	_Trideset_
40	**Четиридесет**	_Chetirideset_
50	**Петдесет**	_Petdeset_
60	**Шестдесет**	_Shestdeset_
70	**Седемдесет**	_Sedemdeset_
80	**Осемдесет**	_Osemdeset_
90	**Деветдесет**	_Devetdeset_
100	**Сто**	_Sto_
1000	**Хиляда**	_Hilyada_
1st	**Първи**	_Parvi_
2nd	**Втори**	_Vtori_
3rd	**Трети**	_Treti_
4th	**Четвърти**	_Chetvarti_
5th	**Пети**	_Peti_

Weights & measures

gram (=0.03oz)	**Грам**	*Gram*
kilogram (=2.2lb)	**Килограм**	*Kilogram*
pound (=0.45kg)	**Паунд**	*Paund*
centimetre (=0.4in)	**Сантиметър**	*Santimetar*
metre (=1.1yd)	**Метър**	*Metar*
kilometre (=0.6m)	**Километър**	*Kilometar*
litre (=2.1pt)	**Литър**	*Litar*

Days & time

Monday	**Понеделник**	*Ponedelnik*
Tuesday	**Вторник**	*Vtornik*
Wednesday	**Сряда**	*Sryada*
Thursday	**Четвъртък**	*Chetvartak*
Friday	**Петък**	*Petak*
Saturday	**Събота**	*Sabota*
Sunday	**Неделя**	*Nedelya*

What time is it?	**Колко е часът?**	*Kolko e chasut?*
(Four) o'clock	**(Четири) часа**	*(Chetiri) chasa*
Quarter past (six)	**(Шест) и петнадесет**	*(Shest) i petnadeset*
Half past (eight)	**(Осем) и половина**	*(Osem) i polovina*
Quarter to (ten)	**(Десет) без петнадесет**	*(Deset) bez petnadeset*
morning	**Сутрин**	*Sutrin*
afternoon	**Следобед**	*Sledobed*
evening	**Вечер**	*Vecher*
night	**Нощ**	*Nosht*

Clothes size conversions

Women's clothes	34	36	38	40	42	44	46	50
equiv. UK size	6	8	10	12	14	16	18	20

Men's jackets	44	46	48	50	52	54	56	58
equiv. UK size	34	36	38	40	42	44	46	48

Men's shirts	36	37	38	39	40	41	42	43
equiv. UK size	14	14.5	15	15.5	16	16.5	17	17.5

Shoes	36.5	37.5	39	40	41.5	42.5	44	45
equiv. UK size	4	5	6	7	8	9	10	11